SHONEN JUMP GRAPHIC NOVEL

Rurouni Kenshin™

Vol. 1

MEIJI SWORDSMAN ROMANTIC STORY

D1056239

STORY AND ART BY
NOBUHIRO WATSUKI

CONTENTS

Rurouni Kenshin
Meiji Swordsman Romantic Story
Volume One

Act 1
Kenshin • Himura Battōsai
5

Act 2
Rurouni in the City
57

Act 3
Tokyo Samurai
81

Act 4
Kasshin-Ryū Reborn
104

Act 5
The Fight Merchant
125

Act 6
Face Off: Sagara Sanosuke
145

END-OF-VOLUME SPECIAL
RUROUNI
MEIJI SWORDSMAN ROMANTIC STORY
169

Act 1 — Kenshin • Himura Battōsai

Act 1

Kenshin • Himura Battōsai

HITOKIRI BATTŌSAI !!
HSSSS
FOR TWO MONTHS YOU HAVE MURDERED AT WILL!
NOW IT ENDS!
ORO?
I'VE FOUND YOU.

READ THIS WAY
DON'T PLAY THE FOOL!
WHO ELSE WOULD DEFY THE LAW AND CARRY A SWORD IN THIS NIGHT?!
HO.
!!
NK!
...THIS... IS THE HITOKIRI BATTŌSAI?
KRAK
NOPE.

*A SWORD WITH THE BLADE UPSIDE DOWN.

ORO!
TOSS
I HAVE TO GO...!!
POLICE WHISTLE!
PWI!!!!!!!!
!
THEN... YOU'RE REALLY JUST...
A RUROUNI, YES. ♡
BUT WHY CARRY A BLADE YOU CAN'T USE?
IT SEEMS...
...THERE'S SOMETHING INTERESTING TO CHECK OUT HERE.
SSSHHHH
YAAAA

DMMMMM
WEAK WEAK WEAK!!
WEAK!!
YOU ARE ALL TOO WEAK!
VSH
...THE LEGENDARY BATTOSAI !!
...HE MUST BE...
SO... STRONG ...

THIS IS IT, BATTŌSAI !!
PTT
!!
THK
OH.
ZZZZZZZZZZZZ

UHH...
!
YOU'RE QUITE THE RISK-TAKER.
RURO--
!

READ THIS WAY
FEH!
DISLOCATED BRAIN--!
DIS-LOCATED GROIN.
NN
NN
NN
GASP!
I AM HIMURA BATTŌSAI!
MASTER OF KAMIYA KASSHIN-RYŪ!!
PEOPLE CALL ME HITOKIRI BATTŌSAI!!
JERK
YOU STOP.
TNG
STOP!
UGH

HE MURDERS IN OUR NAME!!
NOW THAT HE'S TOLD US HIS SWORD-FIGHTING STYLE WE DON'T HAVE TO BE SO--
RUNNING WHILE WOUNDED CAN BE DEADLY.
KAMIYA KASSHIN-RYU IS MY STYLE!!
JERK
RK
REMEMBER. NO RUNNING.
TNG
VSH
I'M GOING TO--
KAMIYA KASSHIN-RYU KENJUSTU (SWORD ARTS) DOJO
神谷活心流
剣術道場
YOU WON'T CATCH HIM ANY-WAY.
LET'S LEAVE BEFORE THE POLICE DECIDE TO QUESTION US.

"KAMIYA KASSHIN-RYU."
"KAMIYA KAORU--"
"--INSTRUCTOR."
WE WERE A SMALL DOJO.
BUT WE HAD TEN GOOD STUDENTS WORKING HARD TOGETHER.
ORO?
THE TOWNSPEOPLE DON'T DARE COME NEAR.
ONE BY ONE, THE STUDENTS LEFT, FEARING THE NAME "BATTOSAI."
DAB
DAB
THEN, TWO MONTHS AGO, THAT MURDERER APPEARED... AND NOW IT'S LIKE THIS.

EVEN NOW, IN THE MEIJI ERA, THE NAME "HITOKIRI BATTŌSAI" STRIKES FEAR.
WHY HE USES THE NAME KAMIYA KASSHIN-RYŪ...
AND IF HE REALLY IS BATTŌSAI...
...I HAVE NO IDEA. BUT WE HAVE TO STOP HIS KILLING SPREE AS SOON AS WE CAN.
流心活谷
HE'S FAR STRONGER THAN YOU, KAORU-DONO.
RRR
HUH --?
MM. BUT YOU REALLY SHOULD STOP THIS PATROLLING AT NIGHT.
TWP
A SWORDSMAN MUST BE HONEST ABOUT HIS FOE'S SKILL AND HIS OWN.
YOU SHOULD KNOW WHAT WILL HAPPEN NEXT TIME YOU FACE HIM.
WHAT ?
IS THE PRESTIGE OF YOUR SCHOOL REALLY WORTH YOUR LIFE?

KAMIYA KASSHIN-RYŪ--
--WAS DEVELOPED BY MY FATHER, WHO SURVIVED THE BAKUMATSU REVOLUTION.
HE REJECTED THE ETHICS OF *SATSUJIN-KEN*, "SWORDS THAT GIVE DEATH."

FOR TEN LONG YEARS, HE STRUGGLED TO CREATE A STYLE BASED ON *KATSUJIN-KEN*: "SWORDS THAT GIVE *LIFE*."
SIX MONTHS AGO, HE WAS DRAFTED FOR THE SEINAN WAR...AND LEFT THIS WORLD.

KAMIYA KASSHIN-RYŪ--
MY FATHER'S IDEAL--HIS LAST GIFT--HAS BEEN *DEFILED!*

THIS HITOKIRI BATTŌSAI--
HAS MURDERED TEN PEOPLE IN OUR NAME.

BUT SUCH SHAME CANNOT BE UNDER-STOOD BY A MERE *RUROUNI.*

HEH.

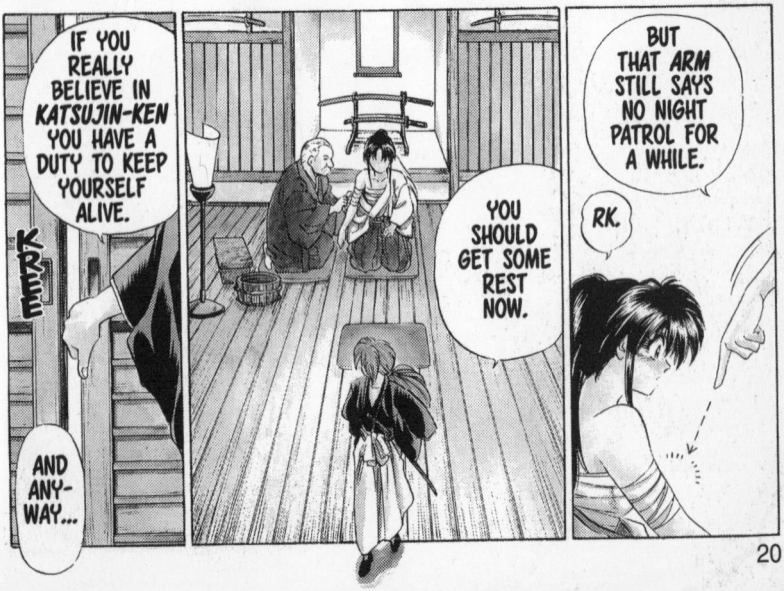
IF YOU REALLY BELIEVE IN *KATSUJIN-KEN* YOU HAVE A DUTY TO KEEP YOURSELF ALIVE.
AND ANY-WAY...
YOU SHOULD GET SOME REST NOW.
BUT THAT *ARM* STILL SAYS NO NIGHT PATROL FOR A WHILE.
RK.

READ THIS WAY
EXCUSE ME.
KLIK
NO DOUBT YOUR LATE FATHER WOULDN'T WISH...
...TO TRADE HIS DAUGHTER'S LIFE TO PROTECT HIS SWORD-STYLE.

THANK YOU, KIHEI.
WE'RE DONE.

I... KNOW...
I KNOW.

DON'T BE TOO KIND.
A *RUROUNI* IS ONE WITH NO DESTINATION.
KAORU-SAN... YOU SHOULDN'T LET YOUR GUARD DOWN WITH SOMEONE LIKE THAT.

READ THIS WAY
A FEW DAYS LATER--
OH.
AN ARREST?
STOP STRUGGLING!
RRG
GRR
COME ALONG!
.....
YOU'RE STILL HERE?!
RUROUNI!
TM TM TM TM
!!
DRESSED LIKE A LADY. YOU SEEM SO DIFFERENT.
OH, KAORU.
HEH

READ THIS WAY
HM? AREN'T YOU THE ONE FROM THAT HITOKIRI BATTOSAI SCHOOL...?
HSS
HE'S VIOLATING THE SWORD-BANNING ACT, AS YOU CAN...
OKAY. WHAT DID HE DO?
MMMG.
W-WAIT~~
I GUESS YOU DON'T WANT MY HELP!
YOU DON'T HAVE THE POWER TO TELL ME WHO I CAN YELL AT!
.....
DON'T YOU YELL AT A POLICE OFFICER!
I TOLD YOU WE WERE FRAMED!
UH...
PAP
IS THERE ANY NEED FOR ANGER, REALLY...?
WHO ARE YOU?!
NOW, NOW... LET'S ALL CALM DOWN.
KIHEI.
DON'T MAKE TROUBLE, LITTLE GIRL.
TRUDGE
TRUDGE
ALL RIGHT, WE'LL LET IT GO JUST THIS ONCE, BUT NEXT TIME WON'T BE SO EASY.

HUH?
WEAK IN BODY AND IN SPIRIT...
OH, NOTHING.
OH, NOT ME!
NYAAA
.....
I DO HAVE ONE LIKELY SUSPECT.
OH... WELL...
ANYWAY, HOW'S THE HUNT FOR THE MURDERER GOING?
SO YOU'RE STILL IN TOWN.
DO YOU HAVE SOME BUSINESS HERE?
UM... NOT EXACTLY ...
THERE'S A DOJO CALLED "KIHEIKAN" ON THE OUTSKIRTS OF THE NEXT TOWN OVER.
A DOJO ...?
NO.
MORE LIKE AN EX-DOJO. NOW IT'S A GATHERING PLACE FOR GAMBLERS AND ROGUES.

READ THIS WAY
TWO MONTHS AGO. WHEN THE MURDERS STARTED.
HMM...
THERE AREN'T MANY MEN THAT BIG. AND SKILLED WITH SWORDS.
A FORMER SAMURAI TOOK IT OVER ABOUT TWO MONTHS AGO.
A GIANT OF A MAN, THEY SAY-- 6 SHAKU 5 SUN.
1.95 meters- over 6 feet
I HAVE NO PROOF, SO I CAN'T DO ANYTHING...
BUT SOON...!
PAP
YOU'LL EXCUSE ME--
KAORU-SAN, I MUST LEAVE TO PREPARE DINNER.
THAT FELLOW WHO WAS WITH YOU BEFORE...
WHO, KIHEI?
HE'S A SORT OF LIVE-IN APPRENTICE.
OH. YES. THANK YOU.

HE SAYS I SHOULD GIVE UP SWORDS, SELL THE DOJO, AND GO LIVE QUIETLY SOMEWHERE.
HE DOESN'T REALLY BELIEVE IN GIRLS PRACTICING SWORDSMANSHIP.

IT WAS RIGHT AFTER FATHER PASSED AWAY.
KIHEI COLLAPSED IN FRONT OF THE DOJO AND I HELPED HIM OUT.

WHERE'S HE FROM?

I DON'T KNOW. I NEVER ASKED.
NEVER ASKED ?!
SHOULD I HAVE ?

YOU DO, DON'T YOU?
THAT'S WHY YOU'RE A RUROUNI.

WHY WOULD IT MATTER?
WE ALL HAVE THINGS IN OUR PASTS WE DON'T WANT TO TALK ABOUT.

READ THIS WAY
SO, YOU CAN'T HAVE MUCH MONEY, RUROUNI. DO YOU WANT TO STAY WITH ME?
OH, NO.
THIS ONE HAS AN ERRAND TO RUN. ANOTHER TIME.
TRUE--
BUT YOU JUST SAID--
HOW FORGETFUL.
EXCUSE ME.
THERE'S MORE?
B-BUT WAIT...
UMM...
THE OTHER DAY...
I NEVER THANKED YOU FOR SAVING MY LIFE.
UMM.
WELL.
I'M SORRY ...

POW
POW
WHY CAN'T I JUST APOLOGIZE?!!
INDEED, WHY NOT?
POW
POW

DO YOU HAVE A FEVER?

KAORU-DONO SHOULDN'T WORRY, EITHER.
BYE, NOW.
HM
WELL, THIS RUROUNI DOESN'T MIND SUCH THINGS.

KIHEIKAN DOJO IN THE NEIGHBOR-ING TOWN ...
OH...I FORGOT TO ASK ABOUT THE SAKA-BATŌ.
OH, WELL.
NO WONDER THERE WAS NOTHING TO FIND IN TOKYO.
WONDER WHAT HIS ERRAND WAS...

READ THIS WAY
HELLO.
HELLO.
OH, SHUT UP! WHO ARE YOU?!
HEL--
鬼兵館
KIHEIKAN
HELLO.
HELLO.
HELLO.
HELLO.
HELLO.
HELLO.
Y-YOU DIDN'T KNOW ...?
AH, SO HIS NAME IS MASTER HIRUMA.
MASTER HIRUMA IS OUT! COME BACK LATER!
IS THE SENSEI ...?
RRG!
"MURDERER BATTŌSAI."
THIS ONE THOUGHT HIS NAME WAS...

WHO'S THE RUNT?
TMP
WHAT'S THE MATTER, NISHIWAKI ?
KAORU-DONO'S SUSPI-CIONS APPEAR CORRECT.

NOT EVEN A RUNT.
GET RID OF IT.

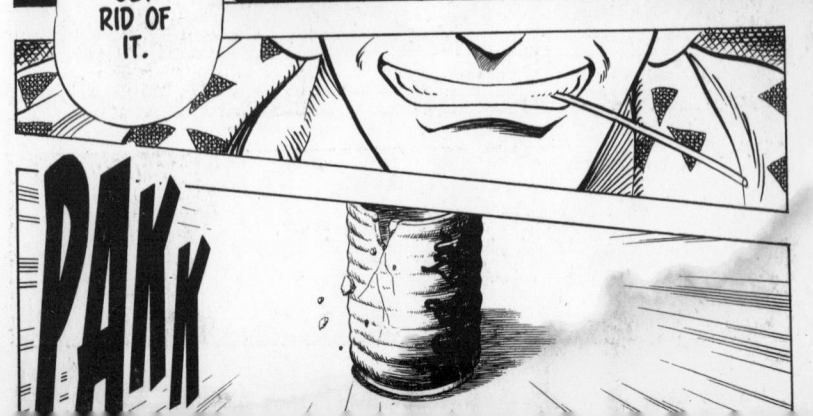
PAKK

READ THIS WAY
EEK
KAORU-SAN.
RRG.
THE CUP CRACKED ...
.....
YES, MISS, BUT...
THE PAPERWORK IS ALREADY MADE UP.
DEED
?
KIHEI, I TOLD YOU I DON'T WANT TO SELL...
IT'S ABOUT SELLING THE PROPERTY, MISS.
KIHEI. YOU SCARED ME.
WHAT IS IT?
ALL I NEED NOW IS YOUR SEAL.
KIHEI?

HEH
HELLO.
Y-
YOU'RE
--
TOOM
THEN THIS PROPERTY WILL BE OURS!
!
TOK
!
VSH
THIS IS MY BROTH-ER.
HIRUMA GOHEI, MASTER OF KIHEIKAN.

I DON'T LIKE TO DO IT THIS WAY.
I'D MUCH PREFER TO MAKE A *LEGAL* PURCHASE.
BUT SINCE YOU'VE CAUGHT ON TO MY BROTHER, I CAN'T TAKE CHANCES.

IT WAS ALL MOVING FORWARD QUITE NICELY, I THOUGHT. THE *KINDLY OLD MAN* TAKING CARE OF YOU AND GAINING YOUR *TRUST*...
UNFORTUNATELY FOR YOU, YOU ARE JUST SO *STUBBORN* ABOUT YOUR SWORD FIGHTING.

THE NAME "HITOKIRI BATTŌSAI" WORKED WONDERS.
THE LEGEND OF HIS TERRIBLE PROWESS IS SUCH THAT NO ONE DARED STAND AGAINST HIM.

KIHEI ...
SO I USED MY BROTHER TO COOK UP THIS MURDER COMMOTION ... AND DISCREDIT YOUR SCHOOL.

THANKS TO THAT, IT TOOK ONLY TWO MONTHS TO REDUCE YOU TO *THIS*.
門下生
神谷道
師範代
師範

READ THIS WAY
MY BIG BROTHER SAYS...
!
NNH
KIHEI...
IT WOULD BE WASTED ON SOME SWORD-FIGHTING SCHOOL.
BY MY ESTIMATE, THE VALUE OF THIS LAND WILL INCREASE 5 OR 6 TIMES WITH THE WESTERNIZATION POLICY AND THE GROWTH OF INDUSTRY.
WHY DON'T YOU USE THE "SWORD THAT GIVES LIFE" RIGHT NOW...AND SAVE YOUR OWN LIFE?
FUNNY.
YOUR MOTTO IS "SWORDS THAT GIVE LIFE."
HSSSHH
YOU COME HERE. OR I GO THERE.
.....

NKH!
KSH
ORK
OKK
NNNNNN
HYO!
VOO
KAH!
!!
YOUR POWER IS ALL IN YOUR LITTLE-GIRL DREAMS.

UHH ...
!!!
THAT IS WHAT A SWORD IS FOR!!
G ...
SSS
TUG
MASTERY-- AND DEATH!

READ THIS WAY
KAMIYA KASSHIN-RYŪ IS GONE.
THIS MAKES THE PROPERTY MINE.
THERE.
SSH
NNH ...
KLAK
H...
POP
HIM...
NISHI-WAKI? WHAT'S THE MATTER?

NNN
RU...
RU-ROUNI ...!
DOMP
!?
HE TOLD ME EVERY-THING.
FORGIVE MY LATENESS.
TUP

.....
HSH
ARE YOU HERE TO TALK ABOUT "SWORDS THAT GIVE LIFE," TOO?!
YOU AGAIN.
NO.
KAORU-DONO MAINTAINS A SWEET, NAÏVE LIE.
SHE SPEAKS AS ONE WHO HAS NEVER BLOODIED HER HANDS.
A SWORD IS A WEAPON.
RU-ROUNI ...
HENH
WHATEVER PRETTY NAMES YOU GIVE IT, SWORDSMAN-SHIP IS A WAY TO KILL.

GLINT
BUT IN THE FACE OF SUCH AWFUL TRUTH...
THE NAÏVE LIE SHE TELLS IS SO MUCH BETTER.

HEY, BRO. IT'S OKAY IF I KILL THIS GUY, RIGHT?
UH HUH.

IF THIS ONE HAD A WISH...
IT WOULD ONLY BE THAT HER LIE WOULD BECOME THE *TRUTH* OF THIS WORLD.

HE'S BEEN A PAIN.
HAVE YOUR GOONS BEAT HIM TO DEATH.

READ THIS WAY
HSH
ALL RIGHT, BOYS?
YEAH !!
ANYONE WHO DISLIKES SEEING THE DOCTOR, LEAVE NOW.
HURTING MORE PEOPLE SEEMS SO POINTLESS.
RUROUNI, PLEASE RUN!!
THERE WILL BE NO WOUNDED...
...BUT RATHER, ONE DEAD BODY!!

ONE... SWING? IT CAN'T BE...
IS THIS SOME SORCERY ?!

NO...IT ISN'T SORCERY...
IT'S SPEED!
SPEED OF SWORD. SPEED OF BODY.
SPEED AT READING HIS OPPONENTS' MOVES. TAKING DOWN MAN AFTER MAN WITH THE LEAST POSSIBLE MOVEMENT!!
--OH.
ONE THING.

HITOKIRI BATTŌSAI DOESN'T USE KAMIYA KASSHIN-RYŪ...
...HITEN MITSURUGI-RYŪ.
IF NOT FOR SUCH A SWORD, THE BODY COUNT WOULD INCREASE TENFOLD.
...BUT AN ANCIENT STYLE OF THE SENGOKU ERA THAT PITS ONE AGAINST MANY..

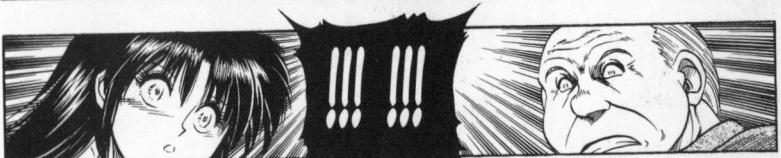
!!! !!!

NO...
YOU... ARE THE HITOKIRI BATTŌSAI ...?
OH-HO!
!
TMMM

READ THIS WAY
UNLIKE YOU, THIS ONE DOESN'T CARE FOR VIOLENCE.
IF ONLY THIS HAD ENDED EARLIER.
QUITE REGRET-TABLE.
I THOUGHT YOU WERE NOBODY THE OTHER NIGHT. DIDN'T EVEN OCCUR TO ME TO FIGHT YOU.
NOW I REGRET IT!
HSSSSS
SSS
...JUST VAIN.
GLINT
OR...
YOU'RE CONFIDENT ...
THIS WORLD HAS NO ROOM--
FOR TWO BATTŌSAI! I AM THE ONE!!

!?
OVER HERE.

THIS ONE HAS NO ATTACHMENT TO THE NAME BATTŌSAI.
BUT STILL...THE LIKES OF YOU WON'T USE IT, EITHER.
TP TP

!!
THUD
NOW. ONE LEFT.

HHH
ZZZ
...THE SHARPNESS OF THIS BLADE?
HIC
BRR BRR
HIC
SHALL WE TEST...
YOUR SOUL IS BLOODY EVEN IF YOUR HANDS ARE NOT.
CHK

READ THIS WAY
THOSE WHO SEND OTHERS TO DEATH ARE USUALLY COWARDS.
RIP RIP
FEH.
ZDDDD
PIDDLE PIDDLE
.....
MY APOLOGIES, KAORU-DONO.
THIS ONE DID NOT WISH TO HIDE THE TRUTH.
BUT IT USUALLY IS BETTER...
...IF THIS ISN'T KNOWN.

W...
EX-CUSE ME.
W...
FARE-WELL ...
B-BMP
ORO ?
WAIT A SECOND!!
GRR
THE LEAST YOU COULD DO IS HELP ME OUT!!
DO YOU THINK I'M GOING TO RUN THIS DOJO BY MYSELF ?!!
I DON'T CARE WHO YOU USED TO BE!

READ THIS WAY
YOU HAVE A CHANCE TO TAKE THE TAINT FROM YOUR NAME.
BEING LINKED WITH ANY "BATTŌSAI" WILL MAKE IT HARDER.
THIS ONE'S HELP WILL NOT BE GOOD FOR YOU.
...I'LL BE MORE CARE-FUL...
YOU SHOULD HAVE CARED WHO KIHEI USED TO BE.
I'M ASKING YOU, THE RUROUNI, TO--
I'M NOT ASKING BATTŌSAI TO STAY.
WHAT'S YOUR REAL NAME? OR DON'T YOU WANT TO TELL ME?
"BATTŌSAI" IS A WARRIOR NAME, RIGHT?
BUT...
BEFORE YOU GO TELL ME YOUR NAME.
GASP
F-FORGET IT! IF YOU WANT TO GO, GO!

READ THIS WAY
KENSHIN.
RATTLE

HIMURA KENSHIN.
THAT IS MY NAME... TODAY.

THIS ONE IS WEARY FROM TRAVELING.
THIS TALE BEGINS--
AS A RUROUNI, ONE NEVER KNOWS WHEN OR WHERE ONE WILL BE OFF TO NEXT...

--IN TOKYO IN THE 11TH YEAR OF MEIJI--
--WITH THE ARRIVAL OF THE RUROUNI, KENSHIN.
...BUT PLEASE EXCUSE THE INTRUSION FOR A LITTLE WHILE.
HEY... WAIT A MINUTE...
PING
IF YOU'RE A WARRIOR FROM THE BAKU-MATSU--
JUST HOW OLD ARE YOU?!
ORO?
AND WHAT'S "ORO" MEAN, ANYWAY?! YOU CAN'T BE OVER 30!! WITH A FACE LIKE THAT?!
EEEEEEEEEEEEEK
YOU DON'T KNOW YOUR OWN AGE--?!!
1 2 3--
HOW OLD INDEED...

The Secret Life of Characters (1)

—Himura Kenshin—

Based somewhat on the actual *hitokiri*, *Kawakami Gensai*. Sort of. Except totally different.

Kawakami Gensai was one of the four great *hitokiri*, or assassins, of the revolutionary (Bakumatsu) period. He was short and skinny, and could be mistaken at first glance for a woman. Contrary to his appearance, though, he was clever and clear-headed despite also being most dreaded among all the *hitokiri*.

Master of an original sword-style called "Shiranui-ryū," Kawakami is famous for felling the great idealist Sakuma Shōzan in one swing, in mid-day. Kawakami is nevertheless a mysterious figure, however, as there are no certain records of his other assassinations.

After the revolution–and unable to let go of the idea that Japan should remain closed to the world–Kawakami found himself in frequent conflict with the revolutionary government. Ultimately, he was accused of a crime he did not commit and executed in the 4th year of Meiji.

As I researched further, it began to occur to me that the story wasn't so cut and dried. What this *hitokiri* could not let go of was his duty to his fallen comrades, and to the men that he had killed. It's this that gave me the initial idea for the "Kenshin" character. As for others, there is the selflessness of Okita Sōshi of the Shinsengumi and the mysterious quality of Saitō Hajime... but, then again, who knows.

In terms of graphic design, I had no real motif. The main character of my debut work was a tall, black-haired man in showy armor, so when I set out to design someone completely opposite to him, he ended up coming out like a girl (heh). Not knowing what else to do, I put a cross-shaped scar on the left cheek. Now that same cross marks the spot at which Battōsai became Kenshin...or so I've heard!

Act 2 – Rurouni in the City

Act 2
Ruroun in the City

HIMURA KENSHIN IS A SWORDSMAN WITH NO DESTINATION, A "RUROUNI" WHO'S CURRENTLY STAYING AT MY DOJO.
...HIMURA BATTOSAI HIMSELF.
BUT ONCE, HE WAS ONE OF THE REVOLUTIONARY WARRIORS WHO SLASHED OPEN THE NEW AGE...THE LEGENDARY, INCOMPARABLE HITOKIRI...
ORO!
THOB
OR SO HE SAYS...
...AND HAVE NOW TAKEN POSITIONS OF POWER AND GLORY IN THE MEIJI GOVERNMENT...?
...WHILE ALL THE OTHER REVOLUTIONARIES THREW AWAY THEIR SWORDS...
HMM?
WHY IS HE A RUROUNI...

YOU HAVE A QUESTION IN YOUR EYES.
HEH
WE ALL HAVE THINGS IN OUR PASTS WE DON'T WANT TO TALK ABOUT.
.....
RG
IT'S NOTHING!
AND DIDN'T I TELL YOU NOT TO CARRY A SWORD?!
PA PA PA PA PA PA
OWOH ?

CALM DOWN! JUST TWO YEARS AGO LOTS OF PEOPLE CARRIED SWORDS.
NO ONE'S REALLY BOTHERED BY IT, ARE THEY?
WHAT ARE YOU GONNA DO WHEN THE POLICE SPOT YOU LIKE LAST TIME?!
THEY'LL ARREST YOU EVEN IF IT IS A SAKABATO!

LET'S JUST GET OUR SHOPPING DONE.
YOU GET THE MISO, SALT AND SOY SAUCE.
ALWAYS THE HEAVY THINGS.
NO COMPLAINING!
KLATTA KLATTA KLATTA KLATTA KLATTA KLATTA KLATTA
KIII
IT WORKED OUT LAST TIME, DIDN'T IT?
RRRRG.

IS THIS THE CORRECT ROAD TO THE POLICE STATION?
WE MUST ASK DIRECTIONS.
PLEASE PARDON OUR RUDENESS.
!

LET US HURRY.
THANK YOU.
UHHH...YES. TAKE A RIGHT ONTO THE MAIN STREET WHEN YOU HIT THE END.

...HIMURA BATTŌSAI?

ARE YOU TRULY IN THIS CITY...
ARE YOU HERE?

KLATTA KLATTA KLATTA KLATTA KLATTA KLATTA
SCARED ME...
I WONDER WHO HE IS. I THINK I WOULD HAVE NOTICED...

GAH. I HAVE TO FINISH SHOPPING!
TTTT

READ THIS WAY
NK
KRAK
THE POLICE CAUGHT SOME GUY VIOLATING THE SWORD-BANNING ACT!
WHAT HAPPENED?
WHAT'S THE COMMOTION?
PA PA PA PA
HMM... SO PERSISTENT.
HUF
VSSS SSSS SSSH
YOU GAVE US A GOOD CHASE--
BUT NOW YOU'VE GOT NOWHERE TO RUN!!
MOVE!!
WHAT CAN ONE DO BUT SURRENDER?
WAK
WOK
!!
LET THE SWORD CORPS THROUGH ...

THE POLICE SWORD CORPS. COMPOSED OF THOSE OFFICERS ADEPT WITH THE BLADE--AND TRUSTED BY THE GOVERNMENT TO CARRY ONE.
TM
TMM
TMM
TM
...OR OUR BLADES WILL MOVE YOU!
THERE'S REALLY NO NEED FOR THE SWORD CORPS TO...
BUT THE MAN HASN'T DRAWN HIS SWORD, AND WE HAVE HIM SURROUNDED.
GOOD JOB. WE WILL TAKE CARE OF IT. YOU ARE DISMISSED.
ZIP
LIEU-TENANT UJIKI...
A 3RD LIEU-TENANT WOULD TELL A VETERAN FROM SATSUMA WHAT TO DO?
WHEN I TELL YOU TO LEAVE, YOU LEAVE.
TH
OK
!!!

WHAT IS THIS?
SUCH A GENTLE-LOOKING MAN.
FYOOOOOO
GASP
OH!

THIS ONE DOES NOT CARRY A SWORD...
...MERELY TO FLAUNT IT AS A SYMBOL OF UNDESERVED POWER.

DRAW YOUR SWORD, GENTLE MAN.
YOU MUST BE CONFIDENT TO BE CARRYING A SWORD HERE.

HUF
HUF
HUF
KENSHIN!
TM TM TM TM
TM TM TM
HMPH.
TOK
KAORU-DONO, STAY AWAY!!
...IS WITH HIM?
HM?
SHE...
HUH?
TASSHI

I'LL SAY IT AGAIN-- DRAW YOUR SWORD.
FFF
IT WILL BE MORE EMBARRASSING WHEN WE CUT HER KIMONO.
PERMITTED TO CARRY A SWORD.
A SWORDSMAN WHO CAN KILL PEOPLE LEGALLY.
AN OFFICER.
ARE YOU...
.....
WHAT'S THE MATTER? YOU AREN'T GOING TO DRAW?
...REALLY A POLICEMAN ?
BOOO
YOU AREN'T A GOD!
BOO
YOU TYRANT!
GO BACK TO SATSUMA!

READ THIS WAY
.....!
HSST
DRAW YOUR SWORDS!
SHIN
DISCIPLINE EVERY ONE OF THEM.
COURAGE IN NUMBERS, HM?
THIS IS NOW A CASE OF OBSTRUCTION OF JUSTICE.
KILL.
IF ANY RESIST...
EEE
EEE
EEE
EEE
EEE
AAA!
YAAA!

ON ANY OF THESE CITIZENS.
DO NOT LAY A SINGLE BLADE...
SLA
SHI
THIS ONE IS YOUR OPPONENT.
IF YOU WANT DEATH, COME FORWARD.
HEH
TO STAY IN PRACTICE I NEED TO KILL SOMEONE EVERY ONCE IN A WHILE!!!
WHATEVER I DO NOW IS CLEARLY SELF-DEFENSE.
AT LAST, HE TAKES THE BAIT.
CHK

THEN IT WAS A HOAX...?
YES.
IT IS TRUE THAT HE KILLED MANY IN EARNING THE NAME "HITOKIRI BATTŌSAI"...
BUT NEVER ONCE DID HE WIELD HIS SWORD IN SELF-INTEREST. ALL HE DID, HE DID FOR THE EMPEROR AND THE NEW ERA.
BUT HAD I THOUGHT IT OUT, I'D HAVE REALIZED THAT HIMURA WOULD NEVER USE HIS SWORD IN SUCH A MAD WAY.
室長署
I WAS DELAYED BY THE MOPPING UP OF THE SEINAN WAR.
WHEN WE INTERROGATED THE CULPRITS, THEY SAID, "THE *REAL* ONE GOT US."
WELL...WE FOUND THE CULPRITS OF THE HOAX TIED UP IN FRONT OF POLICE HEADQUARTERS EARLY ONE MORNING... WE DON'T KNOW WHO ARRESTED THEM. BUT...
SSSSS
SKRAK
HE SAVED THE LIVES OF MANY OF OUR WARRIORS.
WITHOUT HIM, THE REVOLUTION WOULD NOT HAVE SUCCEEDED.
WHAT ...?!
OF COURSE, IT'S PROBABLY A *LIE*, BUT STILL...
PWIK

UJIKI. IS HE CAUSING TROUBLE AGAIN?!
SWORD CORPS? I HAVEN'T HEARD OF THIS.
I'M IN A MEETING, FOOL! AT LEAST KNOCK!!
MY APOLOGIES, SIR...
BUT THE SWORD CORPS IS...
BAM!!
CHIEF!! THERE'S AN INCIDENT !!
REVOLUTIONARIES WERE DIVIDED INTO FIVE CATEGORIES ACCORDING TO THEIR ORIGINS: SATSUMA (NOW KAGOSHIMA), CHŌSHŪ (YAMAGUCHI), TOSA (KŌCHI), HIZEN (SAGA), AND "OTHER" (MITO, FUKUOKA, ETC.).
BUT THEY ARE ALL BRUTAL MEN, AND THE CAPTAIN IS A REVOLUTIONARY WARRIOR FROM SATSUMA. IT'S TOO MUCH FOR ME TO HANDLE.
WE FORMED THEM TO HANDLE THIS "BATTŌSAI" INCIDENT...
WELL... UMM...
SO WHAT DID HE DO THIS TIME?
BY JUST ONE SWORDSMAN.
THEY'RE GETTING BEATEN.
INDEED. A HERO FROM SATSUMA MUST SHOW OFF, MUSTN'T HE?
SATSUMA AND CHŌSHŪ WERE THEN THE TWO GREATEST FORCES WITHIN THE MEIJI GOVERNMENT...
...SATSUMA IN THE POLICE FORCE AND CHŌSHŪ IN THE ARMY, DOMINATING THEM LIKE FEUDAL FIEFDOMS.

SHAK
BUT IT'S TRUE!
WHAT? THAT'S IMPOSSIBLE!
THEY'RE THE FINEST SWORDSMEN IN OUR DEPARTMENT !!
...AND HE HAS A SCAR LIKE A CROSS ON HIS CHEEK.
BUT HIS SWORD'S FASTER THAN THE EYE CAN SEE...
HE'S SHORT... SKINNY... YOUNG-LOOKING...
WE DON'T KNOW.
UNBELIEV-ABLE... WHO IS THIS MAN?
HIMURA ...!
KLATTA KLATTA KLATTA KLATTA KLATTA KLATTA KLATTA

RRR --
ONE LEFT.
OH...!

YAY
YAY
YAY
THEN WE CAN END THIS.
AND YOU MAY ARREST THIS ONE FOR VIOLATING THE SWORD-BANNING ACT.
SWEAR THAT YOU WILL NOT TYRANNIZE YOUR PEOPLE ANY LONGER.
AAA!
KYA
HIS STANCE...!
SILENCE!
I CANNOT BOW TO YOU!!!
JIGEN-RYŪ IS A STYLE OF UN-MATCHED POWER.
EXCEPT ...
A DEAD FOOL.
UJIKI, STOP! YOU'RE--
HE'S A MASTER OF JIGEN-RYŪ!

HYOHH!
DMM
...IN THE FACE OF HITEN MITSURUGI-RYU.
VISSH

LET'S GO GRAB A DRINK!
ORO!
!
GOOD JOB, MAN!
SHWOOSH
WHERE ARE YOU FROM?!
KENSHIN!
TM TM TM
ARE YOU ALL RIGHT?
HIMURA.
CHIEF, PLEASE HAVE THE PEOPLE MOVE ALONG.
RIGHT!
THE YAMAGATA...? REALLY...?
FOR TEN YEARS I'VE SOUGHT YOU...
YOU'VE GROWN A MUSTACHE, YAMAGATA-SAN.
I'VE FINALLY FOUND YOU.
TUP

GENERAL OF THE REVOLUTIONARY ARMY'S "KIHEITAI"...NOW GENERAL OF THE ARMY'S GROUND TROOPS...
THE REVOLUTIONARY WARRIOR, YAMAGATA ARITOMO!
HEY, MAN, BEAT THESE GUYS, TOO!
TYRANTS!
MOVE ALONG, MOVE ALONG.

COME!
MANY OF YOUR COMRADES AWAIT YOUR RETURN.
SSSS
I HAVE A CARRIAGE WAITING.

WHAT ARE YOU SAYING?! YES, YOU KILLED --BUT IT WAS ALL FOR THE REVOLUTION!
YOUR SOUL BEARS NO BURDEN!!
!!

BUT I WILL--
ONLY COWARDS AND FOOLS WOULD DENOUNCE YOU AS A "HITOKIRI"!

MY APOLOGIES, BUT...
...NOT ONE STRAND OF HAIR ON MY BODY WISHES TO SPEND THE REST OF MY LIFE AS A HITOKIRI.

READ THIS WAY
IT'S SUCH THINKING THAT CREATES MEN LIKE HIM.
...SILENCE THEM WITH YOUR POWER?
...THAT WE RAISED OUR SWORDS AND KILLED.
IF WE FORGET THAT, WE ARE NO REVOLUTIONARIES AFTER ALL.
IT WAS TO CREATE A WORLD OF PEACE...
...NOT TO WIN POSITIONS OR POWER...
OH.
HIMURA!
THIS IS AN AGE OF LAW!
YOU'LL ACCOMPLISH NOTHING WITH A SWORD!
--AND THE SAMURAI HAVE FALLEN! THIS IS THE AGE OF BAKUMATSU NO LONGER!
TIMES HAVE CHANGED! THIS IS THE AGE OF MEIJI! SWORDS HAVE BEEN BANNED--

WITH A SWORD, THE PEOPLE WITHIN MY SIGHT...
...CAN AT LEAST BE PROTECTED.
PM
THIS ONE IS NO DIFFERENT NOW FROM BEFORE.
EXCEPT THAT HE IS NOW A "RUROUNI" AND NOT A "HITOKIRI."
.....
CHIEF ...
I KNOW. IT'S CLEAR WHO WAS AT FAULT HERE.
AND A SWORD WORN OPENLY IS SAFER THAN CONCEALED.
SIGH
I WON'T PURSUE THIS.
AFTER THAT HOAX I THOUGHT THAT HITOKIRI BATTŌSAI...
...WAS A DANGEROUS FIGURE. BUT NOW...

MY APOLOGIES, KAORU-DONO.
...NOW I KNOW THE TRUTH IS DIFFERENT.

YOUR HAIR RIBBON. IT WAS RUINED BECAUSE OF ME.
..AT LEAST A LITTLE MORE.

I THINK I UNDER-STAND...
YOU DO?

HE WANTS TO PROTECT PEOPLE, WITHOUT BEING TIED TO ANYONE.
DON'T WORRY ABOUT IT. YOU CAN JUST DO SOME EXTRA HOUSEWORK!
.....
A-RUROUNI. A HERO. BUT FREE IN SPIRIT.
白みそ

CARRYING ALL THIS ISN'T ENOUGH?
DID YOU REALLY HAVE TO BUY IT ALL AT ONCE?
MAYBE NOT.

The Secret Life of Characters (2)

—Kamiya Kaoru—

No specific model here. If pressed, I'd probably have to say the character Chiba Sanako from the novel *"Ryōma no Koibito"*—the self-proclaimed "Ryōma's Girl." There's also that "commanding" quality which I tried to incorporate of Sasaki Mifuyu in *"Kenkyaku Shōbai"* by novelist Ikenami Shōtarō...but Kaoru wound up a plain, regular girl regardless. (Ah, well.)

As it turns out, though, "just plain Kaoru" seems to be working out for now, so I can't complain. Certainly many of my female readers seem to be relating to her. Some of them write that they can't tell if she's "strong" or "weak" as a fighter, but the truth is that she *is* strong.

Kaoru is quite independent for her age, and can hold her own against the kendō masters of the many dojos in town. That makes her at very least a national-level champion. If Kaoru does appear weak, it's only because Kenshin and Sanosuke are so powerful. Whether or not she'll become Kenshin's love interest in the future, even I haven't quite yet decided.

Design-wise, there's no real motif here, either. You could say her look was inevitable. For a girl involved in kendō, after all, a ponytail is *de rigeur*. (Heh.) A blade, a kimono, a ponytail...what's not to like, right? Drawing her is enjoyable enough, although filling in her hair is sometimes a pain.

In that I am a "men, glorious and women, cute" kind of guy, it's true that ideally I'd like Kaoru to be drawn a bit more cutely. "Down-to-Earth" and "poor" are also parts of her character, though, and I can't overlook that. I do wish I could improve the pattern of her kimono, and let her be at least a little more fashionable.

Act 3
Tokyo Samurai

THE DAY AFTER KENSHIN CRUSHED THE SWORD CORPS ...
THE WORD WAS OUT AND THE DOJO WAS PACKED.
YADA
YADA
YADA
WOW! 15 PEOPLE!!
WE'LL HAVE KAMIYA KASSHIN-RYŪ BACK IN NO TIME!
1
2
3...
THIS ISN'T GOOD...

HEY EVERYONE.
HUH ?
SO IF YOU ARE HERE BECAUSE OF YESTERDAY'S INCIDENT...
YADA YADA
THIS ONE IS NOT FROM THIS DOJO, AND IS TAKING NO STUDENTS.
...PLEASE GO HOME.

TP TP
...
GOOD, GOOD.
NOW, TIME TO HEAT UP THE BATH.
HWOOOOO

WHY DO THEY HAVE TO KNOW THAT?!
TAKING ON STUDENTS IS NOT...
GGGGGG
ONCE I'VE GOT 'EM IN, I'LL MAKE SURE THEY STAY!!
THAT WOULD BE DIS-HONEST.
OOM
LOK
IDIOT!
WHY DID YOU SEND THEM HOME?!!
IAF

ARE YOU STILL MAD?
15 STUDENTS! 15 STUDENTS!
AARGH!

JUST HAVE PATIENCE, AND OPTI-MISM!
THERE'S NO NEED TO RUSH.

THAT'S NOT WHAT YOU WANT.
BUT THRILL-SEEKERS LIKE THAT NEVER LAST EVEN SIX MONTHS.
... RRR

TM TM TM TM TM TM TM TM
MY SKILL WITH A PRACTICE SWORD IS LACKING.
AND YOU WON'T SPAR WITH ME!
BUT I CAN'T DO ANY TRAINING WITHOUT VISITING SOMEBODY ELSE'S DOJO, BECAUSE I DON'T HAVE ANY STUDENTS TO TRAIN WITH!

ORO!
B
MP

THIS IS YOUR WALLET, YEAH?!!
KENSHIN-- THIS KID'S A PICK-POCKET!!
TINKLE

STOP!
HO!

LEGGO!
LET ME GO, UGLY !!
ARRH
WH...
WHO'RE YOU CALLING UGLY, STUPID?!
YOW!
YOW!
YOW!
YOU, UGLY!
WAIT. WAIT.
IF HE NEEDS THIS SO BADLY...
W-WAIT A MINUTE!
LET'S GO.
TP
GGG
YOUNG ONE.
DON'T GET CAUGHT NEXT TIME.

KLONG
!
ORO!
I'M NOT A "YOUNG ONE"!!
I'M MYŌJIN YAHIKO-- TOKYO SAMURAI!
I HAVEN'T FALLEN FAR ENOUGH TO BE PITIED BY STRANGERS!!
I'M NOT A YOUNG ONE!!
YOUNG ONE...
I WAS JUST TESTING YOU BECAUSE YOU HAD A SWORD!
DON'T GET THE WRONG IDEA!
MRR...
YOU LOOK LIKE A CHILD BUT IT'S OBVIOUS THAT YOUR SOUL IS MATURE.
SORRY. DIDN'T MEAN TO UNDER-ESTIMATE YOU.

READ THIS WAY
I'D SAY HE'S A BRAT.
WOULD YOU SAY HE'S PROUD OR ASHAMED?
TM TM TM
.....
HMPH.
IF THE WORLD WERE LIKE IT WAS, HE'D HAVE JOINED THE TRULY GREAT SAMURAI...
POOR BOY...
HEH
WE HAD TO GO LOOKING FOR YOU, YAHIKO.
SHFF
HEY. THERE HE IS.

READ THIS WAY
THIS MONTH'S PAYMENT IS DUE.
ZIP
BETTER GIVE IT UP.
HUH?
FORGET IT.
NO MORE STEALING.
I CUT MY TIES TO YOU GANGSTERS AS OF TODAY.
HOOK!
?!
G-GASUKE-SAN...
FWIP
BRRRK
THUD

"YOU LOOK LIKE A CHILD BUT IT'S OBVIOUS THAT YOUR SOUL IS MATURE."

MMM... THAT WAS A GOOD SWEAT.
NOW I'LL JUST GET HOME, HAVE SOME TEA, AND...
HEY, I WONDER IF KENSHIN FIRED UP THE BATH?
K-KLON
K-KLAK
HE WENT HOME EARLY, SO HE SHOULD ...
HUH.
関東集英組
HNH.
STUBBORN PUNK.
PLIP
PLIP
KGOOO
THAT'S ...!

READ THIS WAY
OR THERE WON'T BE ANYTHING LEFT TO *APOLOGIZE.*
EASE UP FOR A MINUTE, GASUKE.
YEAH RIGHT
ALL YOU GOT TO SAY IS *YOU'RE SORRY.*
BOSS ...

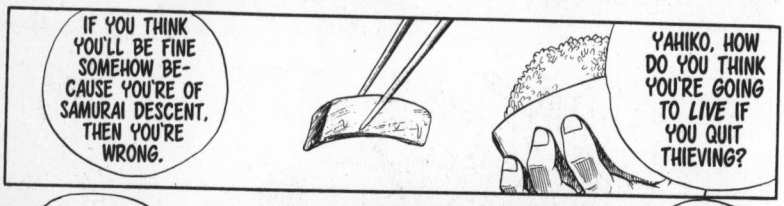
IF YOU THINK YOU'LL BE FINE SOMEHOW BECAUSE YOU'RE OF SAMURAI DESCENT, THEN YOU'RE WRONG.
YAHIKO, HOW DO YOU THINK YOU'RE GOING TO *LIVE* IF YOU QUIT THIEVING?

WHEN SAMURAI HANG ON TO THEIR PRIDE, IT ONLY PULLS THEM DOWN DEEPER.
PRIDE ISN'T WORTH A THING.
THIS NEW WORLD OF OURS IS ALL ABOUT *MONEY.*

IT'S PITIFUL.
AAAAA
AND WHENEVER A GANG OF BANDITS IS CAUGHT, YOU KNOW WHO *THEY* WERE IN FORMER LIFE.
THE BROTHELS ARE OVERFLOWING WITH THE WIVES AND DAUGHTERS OF "PROUD" SAMURAI.

FORGET THIS "NOBLE LINEAGE," YAHIKO. LEARN TO LIVE A HUMBLE LIFE.
THEN I'LL TAKE YOU IN. TANISHI'S MAN...THAT'S SOMETHING TO BE PROUD OF.
DON'T MAKE ME REPEAT IT:
I DECLINE.
PEH

WHO ARE YOU SPITTIN' AT?! THE BOSS WHO TOOK CARE O'YOU SINCE YOUR PARENTS DIED?!
YOU DOG!
HACH
HACH
DOOD

DON'T LIE TO YOUR-SELF.
YOU CALL YOURSELF A SAMURAI, BUT WHAT DID YOUR DAD EVER HAVE? THREE ACRES AND TWO SERVANTS!
AND THEN THE MORON TRIED TO FIGHT THE REVOLUTION AND GOT HIMSELF KILLED!
YOUR MOTHER HAD TO SELL HER BODY IN A BROTHEL AND DIED OF SYPHILIS!
WHICH DO YOU TAKE AFTER? THE FOOL OR THE WHORE?

GOMP!!
!
SHUT UP!!
.....
.....
MY FATHER DIED FAITHFUL TO HIS LORD, OPPOSING A REVOLUTION THAT HE KNEW WAS IMMORAL.
GRN
GRN
MY MOTHER WORKED TO PUT FOOD ON MY TABLE, TO RAISE ME WELL, UNTIL IT KILLED HER.
YEEAAA!
GA-SUKE-SAN!
DOOF

I WON'T FORGIVE ANYONE WHO INSULTS THEM!!
THEY LIVED AND DIED AS SAMURAI!
I'M GONNA KILL Y--
SHING
I'M THE ONE THAT WON'T FORGIVE, PUNK!
D
MM

KROOM
!?
ZUDO
WHO THE HELL ARE YOU ?!!
WH...
IT'S A RAID!! GET THE GUYS!!
!
THEY WEREN'T GOING TO LET ME IN, SO I HAD THEM GO TO SLEEP FOR A LITTLE WHILE.
THEY WON'T COME.

READ THIS WAY
WH...
I AM HIMURA KENSHIN, A RUROUNI.
I'VE COME FOR THE YOUNG ONE.
HSH
WHAT ARE YOU--
AN-OTHER SAM-URAI FOOL?!
I'LL KILL YOU BOTH AT--
ONCE?!

SHIK
WHAT DO YOU SAY?
SHOW YOUR GENEROSITY AND RELEASE THE YOUNG ONE.
BRRR
PLUK
PLUK
PLUK
PLUK
.....
JUST STAY THERE AND BE QUIET FOR A WHILE.
WE'RE TALKING.

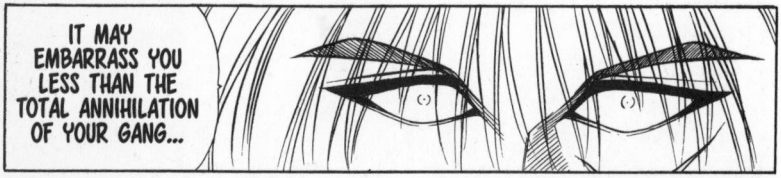
IT MAY EMBARRASS YOU LESS THAN THE TOTAL ANNIHILATION OF YOUR GANG...

YOU WERE HARD TO PINPOINT, BUT AFTER VISITING ONE YAKUZA GROUP AFTER ANOTHER...
ARE YOU ALL RIGHT, YOUNG ONE?
TP

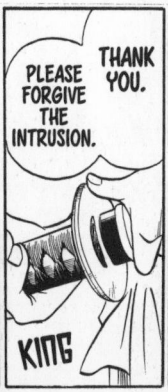
PLEASE FORGIVE THE INTRUSION.
THANK YOU.
KING

FINE. GO AHEAD AND TAKE HIM.

SLAP

I COULD HAVE FOUGHT!!
I COULD HAVE FOUGHT THEM ALONE!

WHO TOLD YOU TO HELP ME?

THIS ONE HAS UNDER-ESTIMATED YOU ONCE AGAIN.
...OF COURSE.

SWOOP
THEN, AS AN APOLOGY, AT LEAST ALLOW YOUR WOUNDS TO BE TREATED.

THOSE WERE THE EYES OF A "HITOKIRI."
AND NOT A HITOKIRI FROM THE YAKUZA. THAT'S A REAL ONE.
I DIDN'T KNOW THERE WERE STILL MEN LIKE THAT.
NO! DON'T MIND THEM!
YOU WON'T GET AWAY!
IF ONE KID IS ALL IT TAKES, IT'S A CHEAP PRICE.
NO NUMBER OF MEN WOULD BE ENOUGH AGAINST HIM.
...DAMN.
DAMN.
DAMN.
DAMN.
DAMN.

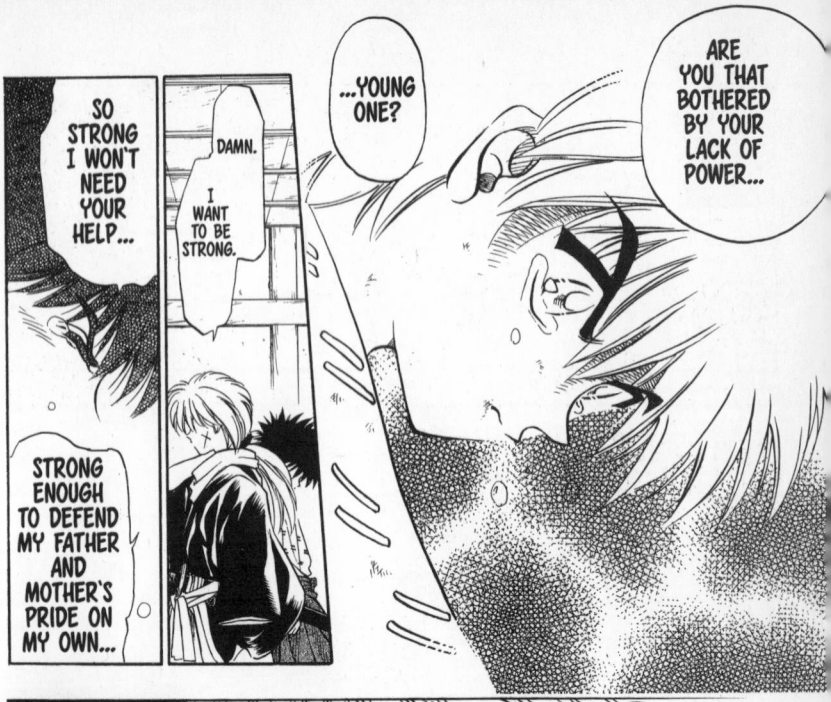
ARE YOU THAT BOTHERED BY YOUR LACK OF POWER...
...YOUNG ONE?
DAMN.
I WANT TO BE STRONG.
SO STRONG I WON'T NEED YOUR HELP...
STRONG ENOUGH TO DEFEND MY FATHER AND MOTHER'S PRIDE ON MY OWN...

.....
OF COURSE ...

I'M SURE KENSHIN'S OKAY, BUT...
...WHAT ABOUT THE BOY...?

HE'S TAKING A LONG TIME ...

READ THIS WAY
SHE'S TEACHER OF KAMIYA KASSHIN-RYŪ, KAMIYA KAORU-DONO.
AS I EXPECTED, YOU'RE WOUNDED BADLY.
I ARRANGED TO HAVE A CARRIAGE WAITING. WE'RE GOING TO THE DOCTOR.
RATTLE
!!
SHE'LL BE YOUR SENSEI FROM TODAY.
GASP
SENSEI?! YOU MEAN TO MAKE HIM MY STUDENT?!
WAIT A SECOND. ARE YOU TELLING ME TO LEARN SWORDS!!?
AND FROM THIS UGLY!?

READ THIS WAY
PAT
THE STAGE HAS BEEN SET...
.....
YEP. ♡
AND SO...
YOU CAN BE AS STRONG AS YOU WANT, YAHIKO.
...THE REST IS UP TO YOU.
...TOKYO SAMURAI MYŌJIN YAHIKO... CAME TO JOIN US.
YOU DON'T NEED TO TELL ME!
HEH!
...THE 2ND RESIDENT OF KAMIYA DOJO...
SHOULDN'T WE BE GOING TO THE DOCTOR ...?
WHY SHOULD I, UGLY?!
SPEW
SPEW
YOU'RE GONNA STOP CALLING ME UGLY!

The Secret Life of Characters (3)

—Myōjin Yahiko—

More than any historical reality, the character of Yahiko grew out of feelings I had in middle school. I was in the kendō club—at first just because it was something to do—but then I got hooked on it as much as drawing manga, and soon I was swinging the *shinai* every day to the point of exhaustion.

The problem, though, was that I was weak. So weak, in fact, that I was an embarrassment to my 183 centimeters of height! In three years of middle school, I was a member of a starting squad only once, and then only because the kid who was *supposed* to be a starter got suspended for causing trouble, and I got bumped up by luck of the draw. Even then, still I was unable to score a win in a league tournament.

The disgrace I felt at kendō, the wanting to be stronger, the still being awful no matter how much I longed to be great, all of that has found an outlet in little Yahiko. Yahiko knows a pain that hero-types like Kenshin and Sanosuke can never know. Of late, he's turned more into a comedic character, but still my wish is to draw him in such a way that, five or ten years down the road, readers can envision him as a great swordsman.

As with Kaoru, there's no particular logic in Yahiko's design...that is, of course, unless you consider that having a defiant-eyed young man with mussed hair is itself a must in a comic for young men.

Act 4 – Kasshin-Ryū Reborn

FOO!!
THEN WASH OUT HIS MOUTH!
KENSHIN, YOU TELL HIM!
PING!
THE HITEN MITSURUGI-RYŪ WILL NOT BE PASSED ON TO THE NEXT GENERATION ...
THIS ONE IS JUST AN OBSERVER.
"LITTLE" ...!!
I'M HERE TO BECOME STRONG!
NOT TO TRAIN AGAINST SOME LITTLE GIRL!
KENSHIN, YOU TOLD ME TO GET STRONGER.
YOU TEACH ME!
YOU SHOULD BECOME STRONG WITH KAMIYA KASSHIN-RYŪ... AND KATSUJIN-KEN.
I DARE YOU!!
I'LL STRANGLE YOU!!
THEY'RE NOT EVEN LISTENING.

Act 4
Kasshin-Ryū Reborn

STOP!!
HYOH!
DM DM DM DM DM DM
YAHKO...
YAHKO...
YAHKO!!
HE'S BEEN SKIPPING OUT SINCE THE 2ND DAY...
.....
KCHING
FILTHY MOUTH, STUBBORN PERSONALITY, AND NO GUTS.
WHAT DID KENSHIN SEE IN HIM?
GOOSH

READ THIS WAY
IT'S TRUE THAT I'M STILL IN TRAINING MYSELF...
YOU AREN'T GOOD ENOUGH TO TEACH ANYBODY!
BOM
I KNEW IF I HID OUT I'D FIND OUT WHAT YOU REALLY THINK.
I'LL BE BETTER OFF LEARNING ON MY OWN THAN FROM SOME UGLY GIRL!

YOU LET ME GO, UGLY!
TAK TAK TAK
AT LEAST I'M STRONGER THAN YOU! COME HERE!
BUT ...
TUG

KAORU-SAN!
BAM
KA ...

...HIRA-CHAN!
PLEASE ...HELP US...

YOU CAN'T GET AWAY NOW--
!
I'LL KILL YOU!
SATŌ-KUN TOO! HOW DID YOU GET THAT WOUND?!
GNK
WHAT HAPPENED ?!
AUGH!
AND WHAT ARE YOU DOING TO MY FORMER STUDENTS?!
WHO ARE YOU?!
VSH
SHUT UP AND GET OUTTA THE WAY.
EW
FY

...
WHAT'S THE MEANING OF THIS?
HUF
HUF
EXPLAIN THIS TO ME!
WELL, UMM...WE RAN INTO A GANG OF DRUNKS IN THE CITY...
YEAH, AND THEY WERE BOTHERING PEOPLE, SO WE TOOK THEM DOWN, BUT...
...THEN THEIR FRIENDS SHOWED UP...
...AND SAID SOMETHING ABOUT REVENGE ...
WHERE'D THEY GO?!
THERE!

!
THERE THEY ARE!

EVERYONE INTO THE DOJO!!
THERE ARE TOO MANY OF THEM!
S...SO MANY...
OHHH

WHAT THE ...?
SHOW THEM WHAT HAPPENS TO THOSE WHO OPPOSE THE HISHI-MANJI GUREN GANG!
HEH. HOW NICE.

BTAM
CRAP.
MASTER HACHI-SUKA!

AUGH!
WELL, WE ARE IN TROUBLE. WHY DOES THIS HAVE TO HAPPEN WHEN KENSHIN IS GONE?
THAT'S WHY I HAVEN'T SEEN HIM! WHERE'D HE GO?
A BAND OF DELINQUENTS--LIKE AN ARMY RESERVE FOR CRIMINALS.
THEY CAN BE MORE DANGEROUS THAN THE YAKUZA BECAUSE THEY'VE GOT LESS TO LOSE.
WHO ARE THEY?
THE HISHI-MANJI GUREN GANG--NOW I GET IT.
IDIOT...
I ASKED HIM TO GO SHOPPING FOR RICE, SALT, MISO, SOY SAUCE...
DO YOU HAVE TO BUY THEM ALL AT ONCE?
THEY'RE NOT AT FAULT HERE.
WHAT DO YOU MEAN, "WE"? YOU FOOLS STARTED IT!
WHAT SHOULD WE DO, KAORU-SAN?
YOU DON'T REALLY BELIEVE THEIR STORY, DO YOU?
I'LL SAY IT AGAIN: "IDIOT."
!?

YOU WERE THE ONES WHO GOT DRUNK AND STARTED ROUGHING PEOPLE UP.
WEREN'T YOU? AND THEN YOU PICKED A FIGHT WITH SOME HISHIMANJI THUGS!
OR MAYBE YOU DIDN'T NOTICE THE STENCH OF ALCOHOL ON THEIR BREATH.
.....!
I'M SORRY ...
WELL? IS IT?
.....
IS THAT TRUE?
!?
BOOM

FUFF
A WOODEN CANNON ...!
HOW CAN THEY HAVE A THING LIKE THAT?!
FUFF
FUFF
WOODEN CANNON: A SIMPLE CANNON MADE OF OAK, LAUNCHING BALLS OF CLAY. ITS POWER WAS COMPARABLE TO NORMAL CANNONS.
COME ON OUT!
OR I'LL DEMOLISH THIS CRAPPY DOJO!
PUFF
PUFF
HYAA HAHA HA! WALLS ARE NOTHING TO HISHI-MANJI!
NOW TO SETTLE THE SCORE FOR MY GUY WHO GOT HIS ARM BROKEN...
WE DON'T DEPEND ON MEASLY SWORDS.
NEVER BE SURPRISED BY HISHI-MANJI.

READ THIS WAY
.....
BRR
BRR
BRR
BRR
YOU GUYS USED YOUR SWORDS FOR A DRUNKEN FIGHT...
...AND HURT PEOPLE?
AND NOW YOU RUN BACK TO THE DOJO FOR HELP?!
BESIDES, "FORMER STUDENTS" MEANS YOU GUYS RAN AWAY WITH YOUR TAILS BETWEEN YOUR LEGS WHEN THINGS GOT TOUGH--
...BUT YOU GUYS ARE EVEN WORSE!
THEY MAY BE CRUDE AND STUPID...
YOU CAN'T GET AWAY NOW.
COME OUT!
DOOM
HEEE!

READ THIS WAY
SS
WHAT THE...?
WE'RE AFTER YOU, TOO, FOOL! AND THE GIRL!
YOU HARBORED THESE PUNKS!
GO AHEAD AND TAKE THEM. WE DON'T CARE.
WH... WHAT ?!
AND LEAVE THESE THREE ALONE.
BRING YOUR REVENGE TO ME.
!
...TO TEACH KATSUJIN-KEN. SWORDS-MANSHIP TO BENEFIT PEOPLE.
KLATTA
I THOUGHT I WAS TRYING HARD...
WAIT A SECOND, WHAT ARE YOU DOING ?
I GUESS IT WAS JUST AN ILLUSION.
EVEN IF THEY'RE OUT OF THE DOJO, THEIR MISUSE OF THE BLADE IS MY RES-PONSIBILITY.
MY FATHER AND I TAUGHT THOSE TWO.

READ THIS WAY
YAHIKO, YOU HAVE A FOUL MOUTH, BUT YOU HAVE THE MAKINGS OF A GOOD FIGHTER.
...SO TRAIN HARD.
YOU'LL TAKE ALL THE BLAME, EH?
WELL, I GUESS I DON'T MIND FIGHTING A WOMAN...
PERV
STOP THIS IDIOCY !!
WOOG!

NOW I WON'T LET YOU GO! I'LL KILL YOU!
YOU BRAT!
RRR
DO YOU THINK I COULD LET YOU DIE ALONE?
DO NOT TAKE ME, MYŌJIN YAHIKO, FOR SCUM LIKE THIS!
THAT DOESN'T SOUND VERY FRIENDLY...
!?
NOW LET'S CALM DOWN AND WORK THIS OUT.
PERHAPS THE TWO IN THE BACK HAVE BEEN UP TO NO GOOD, BUT STILL. DID YOU HAVE TO RESORT TO A CANNON?
CLOK
KENSHIN!

READ THIS WAY
REMEMBER THE RUROUNI WHO BEAT UP THE POLICE SWORD CORPS BY HIMSELF?
I THINK IT'S HIM.
MASTER HACHISUKA, THIS IS BAD. THIS GUY IS...IS...
AND WHO THE HELL ARE YOU?!!
WE HAVE THIS ON OUR SIDE. PREPARE THE CANNON!
NNHH!!
GNNNNN
COWARD! YOU GONNA LET YOURSELF BE SCARED BY ONE RUROUNI?!
FIRE!
!
YEAH !!

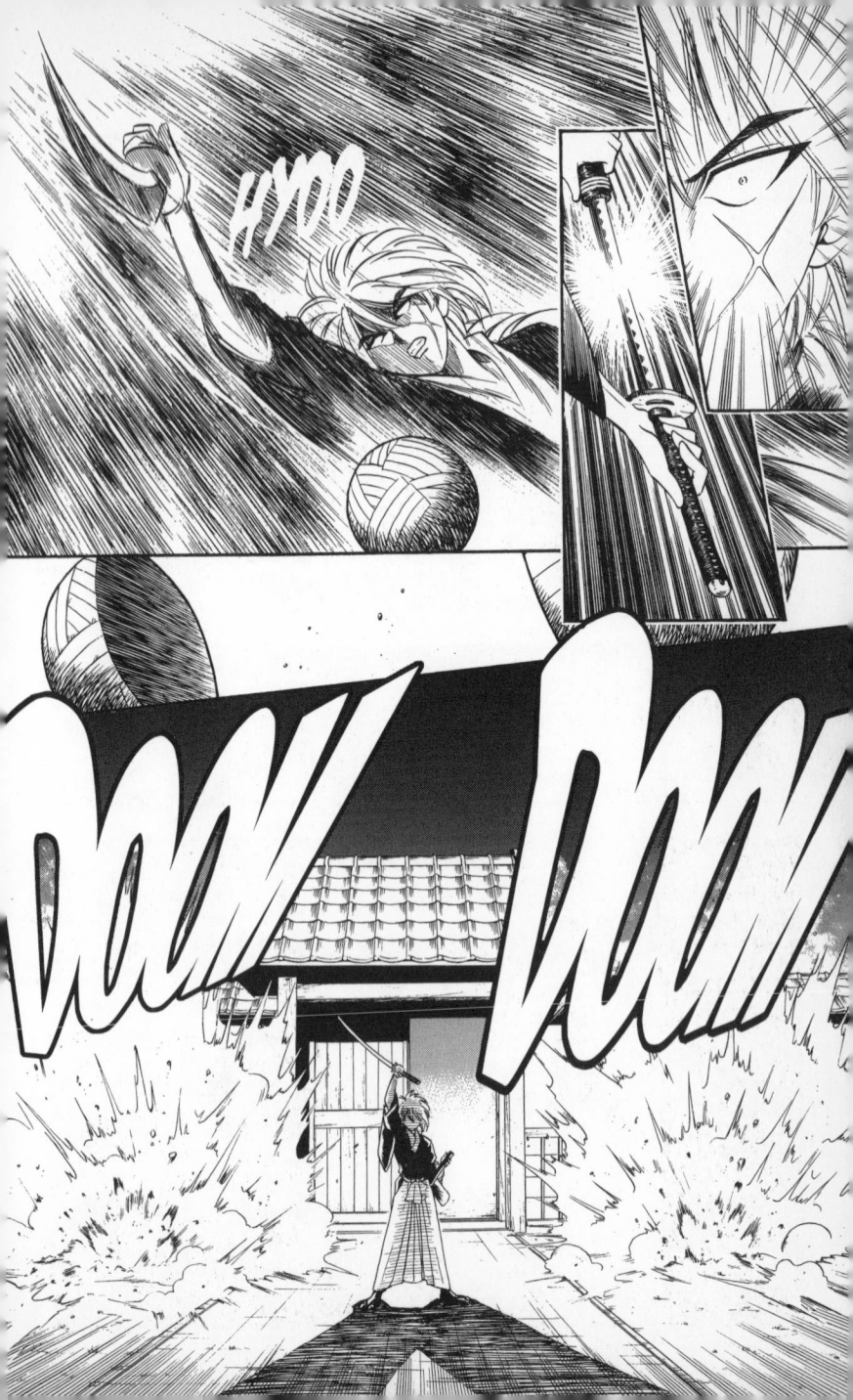
HYOO
DOON
DOON

READ THIS WAY
ONCE AGAIN. STOP THIS FOOLISHNESS.
...WHEN USING THIS SAKABATŌ AGAINST NON-HUMAN OBJECTS.
IT'S POINTLESS TO HESITATE...
.....

SO MUCH HAPPENS WHEN THIS ONE IS AWAY.
MY, MY.

HIRA-CHAN...
PWIK

.....

IT DOESN'T MATTER. GO HOME NOW.
UMM ...

AND FORGET FROM THIS MOMENT ON THAT YOU WERE STUDENTS OF THIS PLACE.
NEVER HOLD A SWORD IN YOUR HANDS AGAIN.

.....
THE WOUND ON YOUR SHOULDER... MAKE SURE YOU GO SEE A DOCTOR...
BOW BOW
PAT
CHEER UP, KAORU-DONO.
...THERE ARE TIMES WHEN YOUR THOUGHTS JUST DON'T REACH THE STUDENT.
NO MATTER HOW SINCERELY YOU TRY...
!
I WON'T TURN OUT LIKE THEM.
QUIT CRYING. IT DOESN'T SUIT YOU.
TP TP TP TP TP TP TP

I'LL ENTER YOUR DOJO.
I KNOW IT'S IMPOSSIBLE TO BE LIKE KENSHIN RIGHT AWAY.
SO I'LL SETTLE FOR YOUR LEVEL FOR NOW.

ZIP
BUT THEN...
HEH
THERE ARE THOSE YOU REALLY DO REACH.

KAMIYA KASSHIN-RYŪ. NO MASTER. ONE INSTRUCTOR, KAMIYA KAORU. ONE STUDENT, MYŌJIN YAHIKO. AND A RUROUNI, HIMURA KENSHIN.
I'VE GOT NO TIME TO FOOL AROUND! KAORU! HURRY UP AND ATTACK ME!
THIS EARLY SPRING DAY IN THE 11TH YEAR OF MEIJI, THE FIRST SMALL STEP WAS TAKEN.
I WANT TO GET GOOD AS FAST AS I CAN!!
I LIKED IT BETTER WHEN YOU CALLED ME UGLY.

Rurouni Kenshin
Meiji Swordsman
Romantic Story
Nobuhiro Watsuki
和月伸宏

Act 5
The Fight Merchant

Act 5
The Fight Merchant

TA-DAA
I FOUND IT WHILE I WAS ORGANIZING THE CLOSET!
MY GRAMPA DREW...
SO I SAID, WE DON'T HAVE TO WORRY ABOUT EXPENSES FOR A WHILE.

INK PAINTING !!!
AHH... DOODLING.

AND NOW WE'RE GONNA SPLURGE AT THE BEEF-POT HOUSE FOR LUNCH!
HEY! I SAID YOU COULD TEACH ME SWORDS! NOTHING ELSE!

I CAN SELL THIS FOR A LOT OF MONEY.
OH, THANK YOU, GRAMPA!
MY GRAMPA WASN'T JUST A SWORDSMAN, HE WAS A MASTER OF PAINTING IN INK.

WOMEN AND CASH.

THE CULTURAL RENAISSANCE OF MEIJI ALSO HAD A GREAT INFLUENCE ON JAPANESE CUISINE, CREATING A VARIETY OF NEW DISHES.
AMONG THEM, BEEF-POT OR GYUNABE (SUKIYAKI) WAS SEEN AS REPRESENTATIVE OF EUROPEAN FOODS, AND WAS AFFORDABLE TO THE GENERAL PUBLIC.
RATTLE
BLAH
HELLO, AND COME ON--
KAORU-CHAN! COME IN!!
LONG TIME NO SEE, TAE-SAN.
YOU LOOK GOOD.
AND YOU'VE SOME UN-FAMILIAR FACES WITH YOU TODAY.
THAT GUY OVER THERE YOUR LOVER?
NO, JUST A GUEST OF THE DOJO.
I DON'T BELIEVE IT!!

BLAH BLAH
BUT THAT WILL BE JUST LIKE SENDING MASTER ITAGAKI TO HIS DEATH.
THEIR HOME SECRETARY, ŌKUBO IS A MAN WHO DIDN'T HOLD BACK ON THE GREAT SAIGŌ!
WE WILL NEVER GAIN OUR RIGHTS THROUGH SUCH METHODS! ONLY A FAR MORE RADICAL...
!?

FOOL. THERE'S NOTHING TO GAIN FROM THE ROMANCE OF "BECOMING A LEGEND."
IF MASTER ITAGAKI DIES, *FREEDOM* WILL ALSO DIE!!
YADA
YADA
ŌKUBO IS FINE. WHO WOULDN'T WANT TO BE PLEASED TO DIE AND BECOME A LEGEND LIKE SAIGŌ?

OH, AND THREE "COFFEE" PLEASE.
WELL, DON'T MIND THEM. FOR THREE, THEN, IS IT?
BLAH
BLAH
BLAH BLAH
.....!
.....!!
.....!

SOUNDS LIKE GIBBERISH TO ME.
ACTIVISTS OF THE DEMOCRATIC RIGHTS MOVEMENT, IT SOUNDS LIKE.
THOSE GUYS. THEY ALWAYS GET LIKE THAT WHEN THEY'RE DRUNK.
JUST A BUNCH OF DRUNKS.

KENSHIN ?
KAORU-DONO, YOU'RE IN A GOOD MOO--
TWIK
WHO CARES?!
PAT
PAT
YAHIKO, HAVE YOU EVER HAD COFFEE?

!!?
SLAMMMMM

APOLOGIZE FIRST, THEN DO WHATEVER !!
MAYBE YOU DIDN'T NOTICE, BUT YOU THREW A BOTTLE AT SOMEBODY!

I'LL SAY IT ALL I WANT!
WHAT?! I DARE YOU TO SAY THAT AGAIN!
KENSHIN !
YOU'RE USELESS!
ORO-RO!

READ THIS WAY
WHAT RIGHT HAS A KID LIKE YOU TO MOUTH OFF AT THE DEFENDERS OF HUMAN RIGHTS?!
SHUT UP!!
YEAH!
GRR
IF YOU DRINK, YOU ARE A DRUNK.
HOW DARE YOU CALL US DRUNKS? WE ARE DEFENDERS OF--
GRR
WHOA. WHOA.
KID OR NOT, I'M TELLING YOU DRUNKS TO APOLOGIZE!
WHAT?! NOW A FEMALE'S MOUTHING OFF!!!
SIR... PLEASE DON'T CAUSE ANY TROUBLE.
UM
UM
TAE-SAN!

!
GSSSHS
OH!
AREN'T THE DEFENDERS OF HUMAN RIGHTS SUPPOSED TO PROTECT THE WEAK?
WELL, NOW.
...THE RIGHTS TO GET DRUNK AND VIOLENT?
HEH
OR ARE THE RIGHTS YOU SPEAK OF...

READ THIS WAY
WELL, I SUPPOSE I WILL "SELL" FOR A CHANGE.
I DON'T LIKE THOSE WHO PICK ON THE WEAK.
I'M USUALLY THE ONE WHO "BUYS," BUT...
OHH!
WHAT DID YOU SAY?!
ARE YOU ALL RIGHT?
UM... YES.
ARE YOU CHAL-LENGING US ?!
ARRRH!
POP POP POP POP POP POP POP POP
STEP OUTSIDE !!
ESPECIALLY THOSE WHO BARK OUT PRETTY WORDS LIKE FREEDOM, JUSTICE, AND EQUALITY.
NOTHING SICKENS ME LIKE A HYPOCRITE!

赤べこ
牛鍋
牛鍋

HE WANTED TO DO IT, SO MAYBE NOT.
WOULD IT BE BEST TO STOP THEM?
WHAT A WEIRD SITUATION...

FOOL!
OH

I'LL SHOW NO MERCY, EVEN IF YOU CRY.
KRAK KRAK

LET'S SEE WHAT YOU'VE GOT.
COME AT ME.
PING
PING

TAKE THIS!!
SHP
!
HEH
COWARD! HIDING A SUN-TETSU!
A BAD THING, INDEED...
...IT MAKES NO DIFFER-ENCE.
FEH...
AW, SHUT IT!!
A SUNTETSU IS MEANT TO BE A CONCEALED WEAPON!!
HOW-EVER ...

AA AA-AAAAA!?
!!
YOU DISAPPOINT ME.
THAT'S IT? EVEN WITH THE SUN-TETSU?
I'LL TAKE YOU ON WITH *ONE* FINGER.
I DON'T WANT TO SEEM LIKE I'M *PICKING ON* YOU WEAKLINGS.
CRIK
PING
GAH!!?

I'VE SOLD A BORING FIGHT.
THUD
THIS IS FINE AS A DRUNKEN BRAWL.
BUT IF YOU'RE GOING TO DRAW A CONCEALED BLADE...
PUNK.
A WHA... WHA...
SHK
ONE FLICK ...

PAY YOUR CHECK AND GO HOME.
BUT YOU NEED TO STRAIGHTEN *YOURSELVES* OUT BEFORE YOU STRAIGHTEN OUT THE GOVERNMENT.
DEMOCRATIC RIGHTS DESERVE SUPPORT.
.....

YAY
I APOLOGIZE FOR THE COMMOTION.
NOTHING TO THANK ME FOR. I DID THIS FOR MY OWN REASONS.
YAY
YAY
YAY
YAY
YAY
THANK YOU SO MUCH FOR HELPING...

GOOD.

IT'D BE TOO BAD IF YOU GOT SERIOUSLY WOUNDED FROM GETTING HIT ON *PURPOSE*.
HUH ?

HEY, SWORDSMAN...
HOW'S THE WOUND ON YOUR HEAD?
MM. NOT SO BAD, REALLY.

SO YOU DIDN'T MOVE. YOU USED YOUR *HEAD* AS A *SHIELD*. AM I WRONG?

IF YOU'D DODGED IT, THE LADY'S FACE WOULD BE ALL BLOODY RIGHT NOW.

SUCH MODESTY.

PFT

HM

YOU GIVE ME TOO MUCH CREDIT.

TMF

LATER.

!

WELL, IF YOU CHANGE YOUR MIND, BUY ONE FROM ME ANYTIME.

I'LL BE AT THE GOROTSUKI NAGAYA IN THE OUTSKIRTS OF THE CITY.

I LIKE YOU. MIGHT YOU WANT TO BUY A FIGHT FROM ME?

I THINK IT WOULD BE A GOOD ONE.

GNG

THANK YOU, BUT NO.

READ THIS WAY
WHAT WAS THAT?
IS HE A GOOD GUY OR A BAD GUY?
OR JUST A WEIRD GUY...
HE WAS ODD...
YOU KNOW HIM, TAE-SAN?
WAIT--!
GASP
HE DIDN'T PAY HIS BILL...
...
KLUNK

READ THIS WAY
HMM. SO ARE YOU TELLING ME YOU WANT ME TO BEAT HIM...?
YES. WE THINK YOU CAN TAKE CARE OF HIM.
左
DON'T SPEAK TO ME AS IF I WERE SOME HIRED KILLER.
WHETHER HE LIVES OR DIES IS HIS LUCK. IT'S BEYOND MY CONTROL.
GLMP
GLMP
CHEW CHEW
I JUST NEED TO ENJOY MY FIGHT, THAT'S ALL.

BUT HOW DID YOU FELLOWS MANAGE TO ESCAPE JAIL?
BY HATRED. PURE AND SIMPLE.
IT WOULD HAVE ALL GONE PERFECTLY IF HE HADN'T SHOWN UP ...
GRNG
RETALIATION. HOW PATHETIC.
MMG MMG
AND THIS KENSHIN-- HE'S REALLY GOOD?
I REFUSE TO FIGHT ANYONE WEAK. MY RECENT FIGHTS HAVE BEEN BORING, AND I'M GETTING TIRED OF IT.
HE'S INCREDIBLE! HE BEAT ME IN ONE BLOW!
FOOL!! KILLING YOU TEN THOUSAND TIMES WOULDN'T BE PROOF OF ANYTHING!
RRRG
PLEASE... JUST LISTEN TO ME.
HEY HEY. DON'T GET YOUR UGLY FACE NEAR MINE.
BOO HOO

READ THIS WAY
IS THAT SO?
THIS KENSHIN IS...
.....!
WORTHY EVEN OF THIS, WHICH I HAVEN'T USED IN YEARS.
YES.
HOW IS THAT, ZANZA-SAN? WOULD HE BE A WORTHY OPPONENT?
HYAH
THE LEGENDARY HITOKIRI... HIMURA BATTŌSAI!!
THE FIGHT MERCHANT HAS BEEN LOOKING FOR A MAN LIKE YOU!!

The Secret Life of Characters (4)

—Hiruma Kihei & Gohei—

The way these two turned out is a direct function of the story. I wanted a pair of interesting villains to start things off with a bang, and figured I'd make one of them "brainy" and one of them "wild." The story of how these two first came together was taking up too many pages, though, so after some thought I made the decision to change them from being circumstantially related to being blood-related. Thus, they became brothers.

Models in terms of design are a certain well-known manager/director from Obata Takeshi's (sumō manga) *"Chikarabito Densetsu"* for Kihei... and some character spotted in a magazine who made me think, "Ooh, *impact!*" for Gohei. (Much more than that, I don't recall.)

Unlike Kenshin and the others, the faces of these two are made of basic, simple shapes, making them that much easier to draw. The closer I got to my deadlines, in fact, the fonder I became of them. Alas, we're not likely to see them again. (Heh.)

Time to draw them? About two minutes. Mm-m...easy!

READ THIS WAY
HIMURA KENSHIN (28)
KAMIYA KAORU (17)
MYŌJIN YAHIKO (10)
Act 6
Face Off: Sagara Sanosuke
HIRUMA GOHEI (37)
HIRUMA KIHEI (45)
SAGARA SANOSUKE (19)

FOEY
WIG
"THE LEGENDARY HITOKIRI... HIMURA BATTŌSAI!!"
"THE FIGHT MERCHANT HAS BEEN LOOKING FOR A MAN LIKE YOU!!"
MNGH
BETTER NOT HAVE GOTTEN SCARED AND RAN AWAY.
IT'S BEEN TWO WEEKS SINCE HE SAID THAT AND LEFT!
WHERE'D THAT BIRD HEAD GO?!
YA A A!
"I JUST NEED TO ENJOY MY FIGHT," HE SAYS.
WHAT AN IDIOT!!
GONN
REAL
YOU'RE THE IDIOT!!
!!!
HOH
NG

READ THIS WAY
A... DIFFERENT ...FIGHT?
THE FIGHT.
NO, YOU TWIT.
IF YOU DON'T QUIT MIMICKING ME I'LL HANG YOU UPSIDE DOWN!
Z-ZANZA-SAN, WHERE HAVE YOU BEEN?
CHING
CHING
YOU WOULDN'T UNDERSTAND EVEN IF I EXPLAINED IT TO YOU.
A FIGHT DOESN'T START WITH PUNCHING AND KICKING.
FIGHT MERCHANT "ZANZA."
A HIRED FIGHTER KNOWN BY EVERYONE IN THE DARKER ALLEYS OF EAST TOKYO.
AN IMPUDENT LONE WOLF WHO DETERMINES HIS RATE BY HOW MUCH HE ENJOYED THE FIGHT.
THOSE WHO'VE FOUGHT AGAINST HIM EXPERIENCE SO MUCH FEAR, THEY SEE THE "AKU" CHARACTER IN THEIR NIGHTMARES FOR MONTHS.
BUT HE'S GOOD!
悪

AKU=EVIL

HENH
HE'S THE ONLY ONE WHO'LL BE ABLE TO KILL THAT ANNOYING MAN.

THAT HIMURA BATTŌSAI !!

HUH?
WE HAVE A GUEST...
TOP

PWIK

HIS CHI IS POWERFUL.

WAIT, KENSHIN ...
WHAT'S GOING ON?
SHP
SHP

UN-CONCEALED ...
BLATANTLY HONEST FIGHTING CHI.

I CAME...
TO PICK A FIGHT.

ON TOP OF THAT ...
...MY OPPONENT IS THE REVOLUTIONARY WARRIOR HIMURA BATTŌSAI...

I CAN'T ACCEPT THAT.
I'VE TAKEN THIS FIGHT AS A MERCHANT. I CAN'T BACK OUT.
TP

THE GUY FROM BEFORE...!

SO IT'S YOU.
SORRY. THIS ONE SHALL REFRAIN FROM FIGHTING.

READ THIS WAY
!!
...AS A HITOKIRI...
...A RELENTLESS ASSASSIN LURKING IN THE DARKNESS OF THE NIGHT...
...HIRED FOR THE FIRST HALF OF HIS CAREER...
THUS THE KILLER WHO WOULD NEVER HAVE SEEN THE LIGHT OF DAY BECAME A LEGEND.
...AND, IN THE LATTER HALF, ACTING AS A FREE SWORDSMAN TO PROTECT HIS COMRADES FROM THE GOVERNMENT'S KILLERS, THE SHINSENGUMI.
...AFTER VICTORY IN THE FIRST BATTLE AT TOBA FUSHIMI, HE DISAPPEARS. AND REAPPEARS AS A RUROUNI. HIMURA KENSHIN.
AND IN THE DECIDING BATTLE OF THE BOSHIN WAR...
THE CHŌSHŪ REVOLUTIONARY, HIMURA BATTŌSAI...
WHOSE WAY IS THE ANCIENT SWORD-SCHOOL OF HITEN MITSURUGI-RYŪ...
...ACTIVE FOR FIVE YEARS, FROM AGES 14 TO 19...

READ THIS WAY
...AND HAVE YOU DETERMINED THE WAY TO FIGHT ME?
A REAL FIGHT BEGINS WITH KNOWING THE OPPONENT.
UPON LEARNING, I THEN CHOOSE THE WAY TO FIGHT.
I WENT TO KYOTO, WHERE THE REVOLUTION HAD ITS CENTER. I HAVE IT PRETTY MUCH RIGHT, DON'T I?
THAT'S THE PROBLEM!
MY RESEARCH ONLY TURNED UP A VAGUE HISTORY.
NOTHING ABOUT WHAT HITEN MITSURUGI-RYU IS LIKE...
...OR WHY THE RELENTLESS HITOKIRI TURNED INTO A RUROUNI WHO KILLS NO ONE.
SHH
SHH
I COULDN'T FIGURE IT OUT.
SO HERE I AM AT THE MAIN GATE, HONORABLY, ASKING FOR A FACE-TO-FACE FIGHT.
.....

DON'T PANIC. ZANZA'S LOSS IS INCLUDED IN MY PLANS FROM THE BEGINNING.
THEN...
HENH
HMPH. THE OPPONENT IS BATTŌSAI. IT'S IMPOSSIBLE.
HEY BRO, DO YOU THINK ZANZA CAN REALLY WIN?

DIRECTLY AFTER THAT BATTLE, WHEN BATTŌSAI'S CONCENTRATION IS WEAKENED, I WILL FINISH HIM...
ZANZA WILL LOSE, BUT HE IS A FAMOUS FIGHT MERCHANT.
HE'LL FIGHT HARD AND AT LEAST WOUND BATTŌSAI, EVEN IF IT TAKES HIS LIFE.

WHY DO YOU, WHO CAN'T STAND TO SEE BULLIES OR BE ONE...
...WORK AS A PROFESSIONAL FIGHTER?
AND WHY DO YOU WEAR THE CHARACTER "AKU" ON YOUR BACK?
THIS ONE DOES NOT UNDER-STAND.
.....
EH?
...WITH THIS, OBTAINED AT THE FOREIGN COLONY...
...IN YOKOHAMA!

WHAT HAS TURNED YOU SO OUT OF LINE?
YOUR SOUL IS STRAIGHT AND HONEST...
BUT RIGHT NOW, YOU'VE GONE BADLY ASKEW.
--NAH.
.....
.....
WHAT, YOU ASK...
IN THE NAME OF JUSTICE CHANGING THE WORLD IN WAYS THAT BENEFIT THEM...
...AND GETTING RID OF THOSE IN THE WAY. EVEN IF THAT MEANS TWISTING AND HIDING THE TRUTH.
THIS "EQUALITY" THEY TALK ABOUT IS ALL A LIE.
I BELIEVE THAT ALL REVOLUTIONARY WARRIORS ARE HYPOCRITES...
BUT I'LL SAY THIS, AT LEAST...
IF YOU REALLY WANT TO KNOW, FIGHT ME AND BEAT ME!
A SOB STORY SHOULDN'T BE TOLD BEFORE A FIGHT.

I WANT TO *CRUSH* THE *HITOKIRI* WHOM THE SONGS CALL THE *GREATEST* OF THE REVOLUTIONARIES!!

READ THIS WAY
COME OUT, YOU TWO.
HEH. YOU'RE A GREAT WARRIOR, INDEED.
SHOW YOUR-SELVES.
BESIDES... SOME VERY DIRTY CHI IS COMING IN FROM THAT SIDE OF THE FENCE.
WE SAID, COME OUT.
HS
ALL RIGHT, HAND IT OVER.
HUH ?
WHAT DO YOU MEAN, "HUH" ?!
AH!
GOOD, GOOD. THERE YOU GO.
THUP
THUP
THUP
.....
BRRRR

READ THIS WAY
LISTEN, YOU'RE PAYING FOR THIS FIGHT, BUT THIS IS MY PROFESSION.
STUPID STUNTS LIKE THIS...
WOOP
...BUT I KNOW HOW YOU SCUM THINK.
I THOUGHT SO. I DON'T HAVE THE ABILITY TO READ CHI...
GNG
.....
CO
KE
...NOT TOLERATED.
...ARE ABSOLUTELY ...
.....
THIS PROPERTY WILL BE MINE YET, WENCH!
...KIHEI.

Thanks for all the fan letters. For a new author, it's sure a lot of encouragement! A couple of you are mailing me every week, and 90% of you seem to be female—has "Shonen Jump" gone suddenly shōjo. I wonder? Anyway, these are the kinds of things I think of as I continue working on the series. I can't quite say I'll ever be able to reply to you, but I will always be sure to read each letter that comes my way. Thanks again for your support!

—Watsuki

IT MAKES MORE SENSE TO ME NOW WHY YOU'RE AS GOOD AS YOU ARE.
IN FACT...
BUT IT'S FUNNY...
I DON'T FEEL AFRAID, KNOWING YOU WERE *THE* HITOKIRI BATTŌSAI.
KINDA.

I MEAN, LOOK AT HIS *WEAPON.* THAT'S GOT TO BE A SPEAR.
ANYWAY, YOU THINK YOU'LL BE OKAY?
ORO?

...SOMETHING *BETTER.*
THIS IS...

THIS ISN'T A *SPEAR,* KID.
I HEARD YOU NEED *THREE TIMES* THE STRENGTH TO FIGHT A SPEAR WITH A SWORD.

OH, YEAH...
WE HAVEN'T INTRODUCED EACH OTHER YET.

MY NAME IS SAGARA SANOSUKE.
I'M KNOWN IN THE DARKER ALLEYS AS "ZANZA."
R.RRRRRRRRRRRIP

SANOSUKE WITH THE SAN OR "ZAN" BATŌ.

ZANBATŌ: A GIANT SWORD INVENTED BEFORE THE SENGOKU OR "WARRING STATES" PERIOD, DESIGNED TO TAKE DOWN A RIDER AND HIS HORSE IN ONE SWING.

ZANBATŌ...!

ZANZA'S FAMOUS "PARTNER."

I'VE HEARD OF THIS...

IT IS THE HEAVIEST KATANA EVER MADE. BECAUSE OF ITS WEIGHT, IT IS SAID THAT NO ONE HAS EVER BEEN ABLE TO WIELD IT TO ITS FULL CAPACITY.

I CAN ONLY USE IT TO SMASH AND CRUSH.

...SO EVEN THOUGH THEY CALL IT A *BLADE*, IT HAS NO *EDGE* AT ALL.

GNNG

IT'S AN ANTIQUE FROM THE ŌNIN STRUGGLE, SO IT'S NOT IN PERFECT SHAPE ANYMORE...

ZANZA FOR SHORT.
...KNEW THAT MUCH FROM YOUR RE-SEARCH.
BUT THEN YOU PROBABLY ALREADY...
YES. LET ME GIVE YOU SOME ADVICE.
LET GO OF YOUR IDEAS ABOUT SPARING LIVES.
...OR ELSE ...
HUMURA "RUROUNI" KENSHIN...
...WILL FACE YOU WITH THIS.
SHHH

HE'S FAST!
WITH A WEAPON THAT HEAVY!
YOU'LL DIE!!!!
URAAH!!

ドッ!!

READ THIS WAY
!
...OF COURSE. NO MATTER HOW BIG HIS ZANBATŌ IS, IT DOESN'T MATER IF HE CAN'T HIT!
IT'S AN EASY WIN FOR KENSHIN!
GRRR

YOU ARE WORTHY OF YOUR LEGEND.
HSSSS
I'M GLAD.

NO... WAIT...
WE'VE BEEN MISREADING HIS STRENGTH...
HE DIDN'T FLINCH WHEN HE GOT HIT IN THE HEAD BY A SUNTETSU.
HIS REAL STRENGTH ISN'T THE ZANBATŌ...
HIS STRENGTH IS HIS INHUMAN TOUGHNESS !!
IT ISN'T EVEN THE MONSTROUS POWER THAT TAKES DOWN A GIANT MAN IN ONE FLICK.

TO BE CONTINUED IN VOLUME 2: THE TWO HITOKIRI!

Rurouni Kenshin

Meiji Swordsman Romantic Story

The "side-story" you're about to read next was published about a year before the current series started. I remember what a hard time I had condensing everything down into 31 pages. This was my very first appearance in *Shonen Jump* magazine, and so of course I put all my soul into it, but when I look back now.... (Sigh.)

For me, the most memorable part was when Kenshin—his name wasn't mentioned yet, but Battōsai's "real" name was set a year before this saw print—changes his tone. My editor and I had very different opinions about this, right up to the very end, and ultimately we gave the character a more "slangy" speech pattern.

This time around, I tinkered a bit with his dialogue, making him sound more as I prefer him now, and still I think about what this story might have been if I'd had two more pages. Once it was finally published in *Jump*, I received mediocre reviews and about 200 letters, and although I was unable to reply to most of them, I'd like to take this opportunity now to thank you for your support then.

—Raikōji Chizuru—

This character is based on the "Chizuru" of Tomita Tsuneo's novel "*Sugata Sanshirō*" (whom else?). Upon the realization that there can be romance not only in saving someone who's being hurt, but in saving someone *before* they're hurt, I longed to write this particular story. Then again, Kaoru and Chizuru are so similar...long-lost sisters, perhaps? (Uh-oh. Guess it would *really* turn into the world of Sugata Sanshirō, then.) Chizuru is one of my favorite characters, and I'd love to bring her back, given the opportunity.

No motif in her design; I just wanted to draw a girl in *hakama*. I've done the sheltered rich girl, the kendō girl...will that make the next a priestess, eh, Watsuki?

END-OF-
VOLUME
SPECIAL (1)
RUROUNI
MEIJI
SWORDSMAN
ROMANTIC
STORY

LONG AGO, IN KYOTO DURING THE REVOLUTION ...
THERE LIVED A WARRIOR CALLED "HITOKIRI BATTOSAI."
HE KILLED MEN LIKE AN OGRE...
...UNTIL HE DISAPPEARED WITH THE END OF THE REVOLUTION.

BUT TIME FLOWS ON, AND NOW...
STOP, DAMNIT !!
TH-TH-TH
IN THE 10TH YEAR OF MEIJI...
HEY! YOU THERE!
HUF
HUF

ORO-RO?
WHAT INCREDIBLE TIMING!
ZIP
ORO?
WHADDA YOU MEAN "ORO"? A DAMSEL'S BEING CHASED! IF YOU'RE A MAN, HELP ME!
ORO?
--WHAT?
AND YOUR KNIVES ARE ANY BETTER?
YOU'RE BREAKING THE LAW!
A SWORD!
YEAH
YEAH YEAH
IF YOU DON'T WANT TO DIE, HAND OVER RAIKŌJI'S DAUGHTER!
WHO THE HELL ARE YOU?!
SHP
TM

HUH ?
PAP
THERE'S NO CHOICE.
HMM... NOT SUCH A PEACEFUL TOWN...
KILL HIM!!
SUH
YEAH, AND WE GOT TWO OF 'EM!!

YOU COWARD !!
VRRRROOOM
GET BACK HERE!!

ORO?
BONK
HOW LONG ARE YOU GONNA HOLD ME, PERVERT?!

SORRY, SORRY. NO OFFENSE WAS MEANT.

PHEW.
SEEMS LIKE THEY DON'T WANT TO COME INTO THE CITY.

YOU LOOK LIKE A SWORDSMAN, BUT YOU SURE DON'T ACT LIKE ONE.
YOU RAN LIKE A MOUSE.
IT'S BEST IF WE CAN AVOID FIGHTING, DON'T YOU THINK?
WHAT A WASTE. YOUR SWORD MUST BE CRYING.
MY SWORD DOESN'T MATTER.
IT CAN'T SLASH ANYTHING TO BEGIN WITH.
THIS ONE IS MERELY A RUROUNI.
HE DOESN'T MAKE A LIVING BY MY SWORD.
A WANDERING SAMURAI.
IN MEIJI ?
I DIDN'T THINK THERE WERE ANY MORE SAMURAI, WANDERING OR...
RURO-UNI?
UNI
UNI
UNI=SEA URCHIN
HM? YOU MEAN THIS ISN'T ABOUT MISPLACED PASSIONS?
WHAT DO YOU TAKE ME FOR?
I DON'T EVEN KNOW WHO THEY ARE!
THEY'RE JUST PERVERTS WHO TRIED TO KIDNAP ME!
ANYHOW, TAKE A LESSON FROM TODAY AND STOP MESSING WITH BOYS.
WHAAA?!
GNG
GNG

FOLLOW ME!
THIS ONE WOULD HATE TO...
FWIP
ANYWAY, SINCE YOU SAVED ME, I'LL INVITE YOU TO THE HOUSE.
BUT THEY DID SEEM TO KNOW WHO YOU ARE...
EVERYONE AROUND HERE KNOWS I'M RAIKŌJI'S ONLY DAUGHTER.

YES, MA'AM...
TP TP TP
Y...
HURRY UP!
MMG!
QUIT DRAGGING!

I'M JUST THE GRAND-DAUGHTER OF A BIG-TIME MERCHANT.
IT'S APPARENT THAT YOU WERE DRESSED WELL... BUT THAT YOU SHOULD COME FROM *SUCH* WEALTH...
KCH

HERE.
WHAT'S WITH YOU?
.....

IF GRANDPA SPOTS US WE'LL BE IN SERIOUS TROUBLE, SO LET'S GO AROUND THE BACK DOOR.
TROUBLE ...SHE SAYS...

GRANDPA...
WHO IS THAT MAN?
TP
CHIZURU.
EEP
EVEN IF IT'S JUST DRESS-UP.
BECAUSE YOU LOOK LIKE A SWORDS-MAN.
MHM
GET OUT!
HE SAVED ME FROM SOME KID-NAPPERS.
HELLO!
UMM...HE'S KIND OF WEIRD, BUT HE'S HARM-LESS.
HE HATES ALL SAMURAI AND SWORDS-MEN.
DON'T LET IT BOTHER YOU, IT'S NOT JUST YOU.
ORO?
I DIDN'T THINK IT WOULD WORK.
THIS ONE IS NOT VERY POPULAR.
MAKE HASTE OUT OF THIS HOUSE.
NO ONE WHO CARRIES A SWORD CAN BE TRUSTED.

WERE KILLED.
GRANDPA'S SON AND HIS WIFE...
MY PARENTS ...
SHH SHH
THEY GOT CAUGHT IN THE MIDDLE OF A BATTLE BETWEEN THE GOVERNMENT AND THE REVOLUTIONARY WARRIORS.
IT'S ALREADY BEEN TEN YEARS, BUT HE STILL HANGS ONTO IT...
I DON'T EVEN REMEMBER MY PARENTS' FACES.
THINK ABOUT IT. I WAS ONLY A BABY THEN.
SO I'M NOT SO SAD AT ALL.
CRY ALL YOU WANT IN THIS ONE'S ARMS.
HOW UN-FORTUNATE.
G
M
I'M NOT HANGING ONTO IT!
OUCH!

.....
I KNOW. YOU THINK I'M COLD.
I CAN'T FEEL SAD...
EVEN IF I TRY.
BUT I CAN'T HELP IT. WHAT I DON'T REMEMBER, I DON'T REMEMBER.
COULD YOU GET SAD OVER A RELATIVE YOU DON'T KNOW?!
SHOULD I CRY BECAUSE MY COUSIN'S AUNT'S BROTHER-IN-LAW'S GREAT GRANDFATHER CROAKED?!
EASY-EEEASY
FAN FAN
ZEE HUF
ZEE HUF
WHEW!
ANYHOW, I'M SORRY.
I INVITED YOU BUT IT DIDN'T GO SO WELL...
NO.
PLEASE DON'T APOLOGIZE.
ALL THIS ONE DID WAS RUN ANYWAY.
MAKING TOO BIG A DEAL ABOUT IT WILL ONLY MAKE THIS ONE FEEL WORSE.

THAT SWORD REALLY DOES NOT SUIT YOU...
READ THIS WAY

WHERE ARE YOU STAYING? I'LL BRING YOU SOME FOOD LATER.
ALL RIGHT. BUT LET ME AT LEAST FEED YOU DINNER.
ORO?

NO, PLEASE, IT'LL BE DARK SOON!

AND YOU SHOULD LISTEN TO PEOPLE MORE...
YOU SHOULD ACCEPT PEOPLE'S KINDNESS MORE.
OH, DON'T BE SO HUMBLE.
TEE HEE

THE REVOLUTIONARY WARRIORS—
SIGH
THEY GOT CAUGHT IN THE MIDDLE OF A BATTLE BETWEEN THE GOVERNMENT AND THE REVOLUTIONARY WARRIORS.
THEY WERE KILLED.
RUROUNI--
SAID HE DOESN'T HAVE ANY MONEY, SO HE'S SLEEPING UNDER THE BRIDGE...
HMM... WHERE IS HE?
TP
TP
THERE'S A LOT OF BRIDGES AROUND HERE...
SHF
RURO —
TP
TP

NK.
TAKE THE HOSTAGE TO OUR LEADER!
I'LL GO THROW THE LETTER INTO THE RAIKŌJI MANSION.
...BUT WE'RE LUCKY.
I THOUGHT WE WERE FINISHED WHEN THAT JERK SHOWED UP.
FSH
AH ...
SHE WAS HERE. SHE REALLY CAME.
TP
TP
BUT WHY DIDN'T SHE...

"RAIKŌJI MUNEIWA. THIS IS YOUR CRIME. YOU TRADE WITH THE EUROPEAN PIGS, ENRICHING YOURSELF AS YOU VIOLATE THIS LAND OF THE GODS, JAPAN.
"BUT WE ARE MISSIONARIES AND NOT OGRES. WE HAVE MERCY EVEN UPON THE WICKED.
"WITH AN OFFERING TO THE GODS OF 1000 YEN, WE WILL SAVE HER LIFE. YOU SHALL BRING THE MONEY TO THE ABANDONED TEMPLE ON YŪKYŪ MOUNTAIN BEFORE THE SUN RISES.
"ALL WHO INHERIT YOUR BLOOD INHERIT YOUR GUILT. WE JUDGE YOUR GRAND-DAUGHTER GUILTY OF YOUR CRIMES.
"IF YOU SCORN THE GODS, THIS YOUNG GIRL'S SOUL WILL PASS TO THE UNDERWORLD FOR ETERNITY. SHINSHŪ KONOE-BUSHIDAN KAITEN PARTY."
.....
SHP
SOUNDS LIKE SOME FALLEN SAMURAI WHO AREN'T HAPPY ABOUT THE GOVERNMENT.
TNG
SAMURAI AGAIN!
BAM
TEN YEARS HAVE PASSED, AND STILL THOSE MONSTERS DO NOT THINK OF PEOPLE'S LIVES AS LIVES.

READ THIS WAY
I'M AN EX-SAMURAI MYSELF... SO LET'S PRETEND YOU DIDN'T SAY THAT.
WE'LL SEND A SCOUT, PREPARE A STRATEGY, AND REPORT BACK TO YOU.
WHAT?
I CAN'T WAIT FOR THAT!
I'M GOING THERE NOW!!
YOU'LL BE RISKING YOUR LIFE...!
I DON'T CARE! IF CHIZURU IS SAFE, LET ME DIE!!

NOW, NOW. YOU SHOULDN'T SAY THINGS LIKE THAT.
FFMP
WOH
HMM. ABANDONED TEMPLE ON YŪKYŪ MOUNTAIN...
WAH
!!

YOUR LOVELY GRANDCHILD WAS SPARED THE PAIN OF HER PARENTS' DEATH BECAUSE SHE WAS A BABY.
WHAT WILL HAPPEN IF SHE LOSES YOU NOW? SHE'LL BE IN TERRIBLE GRIEF...

ANYWAY, WE CAN'T LET YOU DIE.
FROM WHERE ?!
WHEN DID YOU --?!!
FRONT DOOR.
GNNG
JUST NOW.

AND WHAT ABOUT YOU?
TM
THE SADNESS OF LOSING A LOVED ONE...
...NO ONE SHOULD SUFFER THAT TWICE.
HSH
...AND THIS TIME, ALONE.
CAN YOU LET HER SUFFER THAT?
STOP HIM, CAPTAIN! IF ANY-THING GOES WRONG—
VSH
HE'S GOING TO ATTACK THEM!
GASP
THAT MAN ...
YOUR PARDON.

...AND THAT UNMISTAKABLE CROSS-SHAPED SCAR ON HIS LEFT CHEEK...
BUT THAT VOICE AND RED HAIR...
HIS EYES ARE THOSE OF A DIFFERENT PERSON...

IT MUST BE HIM --!!
WELL, WELL. YOU AGAIN...

YOUNG MISS CHIZURU ...
...HAD BETTER BE SAFE.

I DON'T THINK HE'S FROM THE GOVERN-MENT.
PROBABLY SOME SWORDSMAN HIRED BY RAIKŌJI.

HOLD ON.
WHAT ARE YOU DOING HERE?!!

READ THIS WAY
NNNN!! (THAT'S NOT WHAT I'M SAYING!!)
AH, SO YOU ARE. IT WILL ONLY BE A LITTLE WHILE NOW...
HEH
HEH
NNNNN-NNN! (YOU'LL GET KILLED!)
NNNN! (RUN AWAY!)
THE KAITEN PARTY WELCOMES ANYONE WHO WAS A SAMURAI.
WE NEED AS MANY AS WE CAN GET TO BRING ORDER BACK TO THIS COUNTRY.
LISTEN, KID... ARE YOU PLANNING TO FIGHT US ALL ON YOUR OWN?
OR HOW ABOUT THIS...
IF YOU PLEDGE LOYALTY TO ME, I'LL LET YOU INTO OUR LOWER RANKS.
THESE MEN ARE ALL SAMURAI AS WELL WHO WERE DRIVEN FROM THEIR GOVERNMENT POSTS.
IF YOU'RE CARRYING A SWORD, YOU MUST BE ANOTHER SAMURAI WHO REFUSES TO YIELD TO MEIJI.
WE SHOULD ALL BE WORKING TOGETHER.
YOU SEE, WE'RE ALL ALIKE HERE.

RUROUNI...?
!!
ALIKE?
I DON'T THINK SO.
YOUR ENVY IS OBVIOUS. THE ENVY OF THOSE WHO FAILED TO SEE THE FLOW OF TIME TOWARD THOSE WHO SAW IT.
TMP
YOUR BANNERS ARE NOTHING BUT LIES.
AND HOW MANY OF YOU DOES IT TAKE TO CAPTURE ONE YOUNG GIRL?
KILL HIM!!!
JUST CALL IT THE COWARD PARTY.
KAITEN PARTY? WHAT A JOKE.
TKC
...PUNK ...
RRR
YOU ...

!!
VS
YOU'LL WISH YOU'D LISTENED, FOOL!
YOU'LL REGRET IT IN HELL!
DO NOT BLAME ME FOR THIS.
I WON'T HOLD BACK.
HYU

OH!
KYAAA!

WH...
WH...
WHA... WHAT IS HE ?!!!
!!!

READ THIS WAY
HE DID HIS DEEDS ONLY IN THE SHADOWS, SO THERE IS NO RECORD OF HIM IN HISTORY.
BUT...THE LEGENDS SAY HE SLEW EVERYONE IN HIS WAY WITH THE SPEED OF HIS MURDEROUS SATSUJINKEN.
VNNN
ONE OF THE GREAT REVOLUTIONARY WARRIORS.
I SAW HIM ONCE IN KYOTO DURING THE BAKUMATSU.
HIMURA BATTŌSAI?
HE WAS EXTRAORDINARILY STRONG...AND KILLED AN EXTRAORDINARY NUMBER OF PEOPLE.
THE NAME MEN GAVE HIM WAS "HITOKIRI BATTŌSAI."
ALL SLAUGHTERED...
NO ONE HAS ESCAPED ALIVE FROM HIS UNLEASHED SWORD.

READ THIS WAY
SEND EVERY MAN TO THE YŪKYŪ TEMPLE--NOW!
THIS IS THE MEIJI ERA! EVEN IF THEY ARE CRIMINALS, THEY CANNOT BE MASSACRED WITHOUT BEING TRIED UNDER LAW!
N...
NO...
GASP!
FA
SKILL WORTHY OF YOUR BIG WORDS.
ALL DEAD IN SECONDS.
.....
SO.
HWOOOO

YES. THE STRONGEST ARMOR IN THE WORLD.
EUROPEAN STEEL ARMOR...
NOT EVEN THE BEST SWORDS CAN PENETRATE...
TP
YOU CANNOT DEFEAT ME!!
BUT ...
GLINT
...THIS !!

YOU DIE!!
NOW--
!
TOO SLOW.

NICE DODGE!!
BUT YOU'LL NEVER SLASH THROUGH THIS--
NG!

TAKE A BETTER LOOK AT YOUR OPPONENT'S WEAPON BEFORE YOU BOAST ABOUT YOUR ARMOR.
GUG... HAA...
WE'RE TOO LATE...
OHH!
!!
DAMN IT...
PSH
PAK
PSH
SHP
THIS SWORD CAN'T CUT ANYTHING...
PAW
A... SAKABATŌ ?!
NN!

JUST BEING A "HITOKIRI" ...
KN
CAPTAIN, THEY'RE ALL ALIVE!
BROKEN BONES-- BUT NO FATAL WOUNDS!!
WHY...WOULD HITOKIRI BATTOSAI...?
NO WAY ...
DOESN'T MEAN THIS ONE ENJOYS KILLING PEOPLE.
.....
HMOO
DON'T GET CARRIED AWAY!
Ouch!
OH, POOR GIRL. YOU'RE SO SCARED YOU CAN'T EVEN SPEAK...
GOOSH
.....
ARE YOU ALL RIGHT, CHIZURU-DONO?
SHWIP

READ THIS WAY
NOW ...
TP
TAKE CARE.
.....
GOOD.
GOOD.
BRING THAT ENERGY TO THE NEW WORLD WE'RE MAKING.
THAT'S THE SPIRIT WE NEED IN THE AGE OF MEIJI.
PFF
ORO ?
ZOOP
WAIT UP A MINUTE.
TM TM TM

READ THIS WAY
REALLY, YOU NEEDN'T BOTHER...
TING
THIS IS JUST A LOAN, THOUGH, GOT IT?
YOUR HAIR'LL KEEP GETTING IN YOUR WAY LIKE THAT.
DUMMY ...
PAT
I TOLD YOU--YOU SHOULD ACCEPT PEOPLE'S KINDNESS MORE!
THANK YOU BOTH...
TWEE TWEE
BUT... BUT...
I'LL GET YOU IF YOU DON'T!
WHEN YOU COME THROUGH THIS CITY AGAIN, YOU HAVE TO STOP BY.
WHEN THAT TIME COMES, I MIGHT BE ABLE TO WELCOME YOU FROM MY HEART.
YES. I INVITE YOU, TOO.

LONG AGO, IN KYOTO DURING THE REVOLUTION...
THERE LIVED A WARRIOR CALLED "HITOKIRI BATTOSAI."
HE KILLED MEN LIKE AN OGRE...
...UNTIL HE DISAPPEARED WITH THE END OF THE REVOLUTION.
BUT TIME FLOWS ON, AND IN THE 10TH YEAR OF MEIJI...
HEE
HEE
IN TOKYO --
A SWORDSMAN KNOWN AS "RUROUNI" ...
That man's wearing a ribbon.
HEE
HEE
It looks good, though.
ORO?
No clue that ribbons are for women.
...IS DRIFTING ALOOF WITHIN THE CURRENT OF TIME.
BUT IF THAT MAN WAS A WARRIOR IN THE REVOLUTION, HOW OLD IS HE NOW?
EEP!
EVEN IF HE WERE YOUNG THEN, HE MUST BE PAST THIRTY.
YOU'RE RIGHT!

RUROUNI • END

GLOSSARY of the RESTORATION

*A brief guide to select Japanese terms used in **Rurouni Kenshin**. Note that, both here and within the story itself, all names are Japanese style—i.e., last or "family" name first, with personal or "given" name following. This is both because **Kenshin** is a "period" story, as well as to decrease confusion—were we to reverse the order of the historically established assassin-name "Hitokiri Battôsai," for example, it would make little sense to then call him "Battôsai Himura."*

Hiten Mitsurugi-ryû
Kenshin's sword technique, used more for defense than offense. An "ancient style that pits one against many," it requires exceptional speed and agility to master

hitokiri
An assassin. Famous swordsmen of the period were sometimes thus known to adopt "professional" names—***Kawakami Gensai***, for example, was also known as "Hitokiri Gensai"

Ishin Shishi
Loyalist or pro-Imperialist ***patriots*** who fought to restore the Emperor to his ancient seat of power

Jigen-ryû
Aggressive swordsmanship style, characterized by one-handed draws/cuts, and the use of turning. Used in this story by Ujiki, a corrupt officer of the Police Sword Corps

Kamiya Kasshin-ryû
Sword-arts or ***kenjutsu*** school established by Kaoru's father, who rejected the ethics of ***Satsujin-ken*** for ***Katsujin-ken***

katsujin-ken
"Swords that give life"; the sword-arts style developed over ten years by Kaoru's father and founding principle of ***Kamiya Kasshin-ryû***

Kawakami Gensai
Real-life, historical inspiration for the character of ***Himura Kenshin***

kenjutsu
The art of fencing; sword arts; *kendô*

Kiheitai
Fighting force which included men of both the merchant and peasant classes

-kun

Aizu
Tokugawa-affiliated domain; fourth battle of the ***Boshin War***

Bakumatsu
Final, chaotic days of the Tokugawa regime

Boshin War
Civil war of 1868-69 between the new government and the ***Tokugawa Bakufu***. The anti-*Bakufu*, pro-Imperial side (the Imperial Army) won, easily defeating the Tokugawa supporters

-chan
Honorific. Can be used either as a diminutive (e.g., with a small child—"Little Hanako or Kentarô"), or with those who are grown, to indicate affection ("My dear...")

dojo
Martial arts training hall

-dono
Honorific. Even more respectful than ***–san***; the effect in modern-day Japanese conversation would be along the lines of "Milord So-and-So." As used by Kenshin, it indicates both respect and humility

Edo
Capital city of the ***Tokugawa Bakufu***, renamed ***Tokyo*** ("Eastern Capital") after the Meiji Restoration

Hijikata Toshizô
Vice-commander of the ***Shinsengumi***

Himura Battôsai
Swordsman of legendary skills and former assassin (*hitokiri*) of the ***Ishin Shishi***

Himura Kenshin
Kenshin's "real" name, revealed to Kaoru only at her urging

LUFFY AND HIS CREW DEFEND A VILLAGE FROM CAPTAIN KURO AND HIS BLACK CAT PIRATES!

VOLUME 4!

Volumes 1-4 on Sale Now!

Vol. 5 available Nov. 9th!

ONE PIECE © 1997 by EIICHIRO ODA / SHUEISHA Inc. Covers subject to change.

遊☆戯☆王
VOLUME 6
Only $7.95 Each!
PREPARE FOR A NEW CHALLENGER... BAKURA!
Volume 1-6 Available Now!
VIZ
SHONEN JUMP GRAPHIC NOVEL
Story & Art by Kazuki Takahashi volume 6
On Sale At:
www.shonenjump.com
Also available at your local bookstore, comic store and Suncoast Motion Picture Company.
YU-GI-OH! © 1996 by KAZUKI TAKAHASHI / SHUEISHA Inc.
Covers subject to change.

A MIGHTY SHAMAN COMES FROM AMERICA TO TEST YOH

SHAMAN KING © 1998 by HIROYUKI TAKEI / SHUEISHA Inc.
Cover art subject to change.

BLEACH © 2001 by TITE KUBO / SHUEISHA Inc.
COVER ART SUBJECT TO CHANGE.

THE PRINCE OF TENNIS © 1999 by TAKESHI KONOMI / SHUEISHA Inc.
COVER ART SUBJECT TO CHANGE.

Teacher; master

Shinsengumi
Elite, notorious, government-sanctioned and exceptionally skilled swordsman-supporters of the military government (***Bakufu***) which had ruled Japan for nearly 250 years, the Shinsengumi ("newly selected corps") were established in 1863 to suppress the ***loyalists*** and restore law and order to the blood-soaked streets of the imperial capital (see ***Kyoto***)

shôgun
Feudal military ruler of Japan

shôgunate
See ***Tokugawa Bakufu***

suntetsu
Small, handheld blade, designed for palming and concealment

Tokugawa Bakufu
Military feudal government which dominated Japan from 1603 to 1867

Tokugawa Yoshinobu
15th and last ***shôgun*** of Japan. His peaceful abdication in 1867 marked the end of the ***Bakufu*** and beginning of ***Meiji***

Tokyo
The renaming of "***Edo***" to "***Tokyo***" is a marker of the start of the ***Meiji Restoration***

Toba Fushimi, Battle at
Battle near ***Kyoto*** between the forces of the new, imperial government and the fallen ***shôgunate***. Ending with an imperial victory, it was the first battle of the ***Boshin War***

Yamagata Aritomo
(1838-1922) Soldier and statesman, chief founder of the modern Japanese army. A samurai of Chôshû, he studied military science in Europe and returned to Japan in 1870 to head the war ministry

Honorific. Used in the modern day for male students, or those who grew up together, but another usage—the one you're more likely to find in **Rurouni Kenshin**—is the "superior-to-inferior" form, intended as a way to emphasize a difference in status or rank, as well as to indicate familiarity or affection

Kyoto
Home of the Emperor and imperial court from A.D. 794 until shortly after the Meiji Restoration in 1868

loyalists
Those who supported the return of the Emperor to power; ***Ishin Shishi***

Meiji Restoration
1853-1868; culminated in the collapse of the ***Tokugawa Bakufu*** and the restoration of imperial rule. So called after Emperor Meiji, whose chosen name was written with the characters for "culture and enlightenment"

patriots
Another term for ***Ishin Shishi***...and when used by Sano, not a flattering one

rurouni
Wanderer, vagabond

sakabatô
Reversed-edge sword (the dull edge on the side the sharp should be, and vice-versa); carried by Kenshin as a symbol of his resolution never to kill again

-san
Honorific. Carries the meaning of "Mr.," "Ms.," "Miss," etc., but used more extensively in Japanese than its English equivalent (note that even an enemy may be addressed as "*-san*")

satsujin-ken
"Swords that give death"; styles of swordsmanship rejected by Kaoru's father

Seinan War
1877 uprising of the samurai classes against the new Meiji government, ending in defeat by the government army. Also known as the "Satsuma Rebellion"

sensei